©2016 Trina Brunk

Cover photo by Elijah Gersky. Photo of Trina by Amy Jerke of
Papillon Sky Photography.

This work is a gift for you to share freely as you feel inspired so
please duplicate and invite others to do the same. If you feel the call
to contribute to Trina's ability to give freely you may send
donations by PayPal to trinabrunk@gmail.com or visit
www.trinabrunk.bandcamp.com for music and more opportunities
to share from the heart as you are guided.

CLOSER THAN

YOU THINK

Poetry, Practices, Prayers and Passion
On My Soul's Path Home

ℰᏟℛ

By Trina Brunk

Love is closer than you think.

Open up and drink it in!

౷)ౙ

For my Beloved in your myriad forms.
I love you so much!
Thank you for loving me!

Table of Contents

Acknowledgements

Thank you Grandmothers and Grandfathers. Thank you Nature, and Earth. Thank you Elijah, Aidan and Ethan. Being your mom has brought me so much joy and taught me so much and made life rich and real beyond words. I love you so much and have no idea how to express to you what you mean to me. Rob, thank you for co-creating with me and caring for our co-creation; for seeing and honoring the unique hearts and spirits of these sons of ours, for supporting them, and for walking this road with me and growing alongside me. Tracy, this book would not have been anywhere near the book it is without your insight and caring, and my life wouldn't have been anywhere near as interesting and meaningful, either. With open heart and brilliant mind you went before me and opened up worlds that would have been very hard for me to reach otherwise. Then when I considered the questions you asked, even more new worlds opened up inside me. Toni, do you know what your enthusiasm and deep listening and friendship have meant to me? Your bright and persistent presence at critical moments in my life has given me ground to plant seeds of my soul in. You have taught me so much about being a friend, by being one. Your explorations have ignited my own. Tami, your magical presence in my life since we were the Little Girls together has kept me always at least a little bit awake to the Mysteries of life. I am so grateful for our parallel paths, for the synchronicities and the differences alike. Mom and Dad and all my other beautiful siblings, thank you for being my earth family and for forming the context that I have learned and grown so much through. To my Ancestors, Grandmothers and Grandfathers, thank you, thank you, thank you for your wisdom and guidance and for kicking my butt when it needed kicking; for patiently teaching me and loving me as I make my way in this world. Douglas, our love rocks my world and opens my heart and blows my mind. Being with you has taught me how sweet a low pace can be and how many interesting places are there to explore and savor, when I slow down. Elizabeth Klug, aaah, beautiful Coyote Woman, Sister, Teacher, Playmate, Friend! Thank you for praying with me and singing with me and falling in love with God with me again and again. Life becomes so much more than it was before, with you in it! Michelle Johnstone, so much luminescence in you, I am so grateful that you are my friend. Thank you for all of your support and your Presence and your wisdom. Anabhra, my dear sacred friend, thank you for the initiation into a whole 'nother paradigm. Thank you for standing by me and helping me face the pain when that was all there was left to do, and for being my friend in all the other times. Ashley Phillips, I cannot think of you without smiling in delight. You have been there with me in some of the best times and the hardest times and given me just the word or phrase I needed to turn my whole perspective around. You have been my Fairy God Friend in ways that continue to expand me and blow my mind. You always nail it, in the very best way possible. And your shoulder seems to have magical properties, which I won't mention here. Tasha Huesca, your humble grace and wisdom have gently helped me see my arrogance and blind spots, and your strength and creativity and passion inspire me. Amy Jerke, thank you for being such a gift during those early SoulPath Circles, and for the essences you made, and for the beauty you bring to whatever you touch, including my photos. Patricia Bleecker, you were a true friend to me when I had no idea what that meant or how to respond in kind. The memory of your loyalty stays with me and I hope I get to reconnect with you someday so I can tell you. Paul Janeczek, wherever you are, thank you for really paying attention to me. Hummingbird Community and especially Rich, Marie, Katharine, Makasha, Ralph, Sara, Jasmyne, Dabo and Linda: you were my first Circle of Light on planet Earth and I love you so much. Thank you for loving me and feeding my soul and teaching me about co-creativity and community and the Field, and showing me another way to live. Laura Adair, your support came in magical ways again and again when the need was profound, and the only one I was asking for support from was Spirit. Thank you from the bottom of my heart for showing up as Spirit with skin on. Masako Ogawa, our work together taught me so much. Thank you for your insistence that my work is good, and for your commitment to your path and for showing up even when it was hard. Badger and Darcy and Ben and Sam, thank you for holding up a new possibility that helped me see love in a new way. Infinite thanks to the coco community, to the folks in various stages of re-emergence who are deliberately and persistently showing up in the name of mutual liberation: your attention is a brilliant and beautiful gift. I thank my dear friends at the Green Dragon community. Thank you for being there and being you and for giving me a place in your hearts and on your land to come Home to for a while. Chris Fischer, thank you for being there and being my Friend and through your practical wisdom helping me ground myself and cut through the bullshit while simultaneously exploring crazy outer edges with me! PJ and the folks at Renew Missouri, thank you for giving something new a shot, for being open minded and creative as well as intelligent and doing such fabulous work. Amber Sparks, thank you for your soul friendship and your eagle eyes!

To the contributors of this CD and Book project, the ones who pre-bought copies and gave generously from their hearts: Laura Adair, Tracy Barnett, Mellodie Wilson, Tanya Oliphant, Sharon Allmond, Robert Ashbaugh, Emily Cooke, Shay DuBois, Mary Dressel, Jackie Noel, PJ Wilson, Marcia K Nelson, Elizabeth Klug,

Closer Than You Think

Judy Brunk, John MacEnulty, Grant Paris, Carol Buckels, Michael Stacy, Evelyn Brown, Luna Langer, Kara Kulpa, Kimberly Thompson, Roger Mock, Denise Nyby, Dennis Heck, Mary Clements, Charlet Quay, Douglas Huajardo, Kay Losciuto, Amber Sparks, Laurie Peters, Michelle Johnstone, Kristin Powell, Kevin Hicks, Tami Brunk, Stan Anderson, Megan Farmer, Julie Peterson, Kim Woodward, Toni Rahman, James McCown, Elisa Booth, Chad Mast, Alicia Adams, Megan Hall, Judy Brunk, Sally DuBane, Andy Grall: to all of you I am grateful beyond words! thank you for being who you are and for sharing the gifts of your abundance to support the expression of my gifts.

And thank you, most of all, to the Infinite Source of my existence for this journey into the Mystery and for my eternal connection with you.

Introduction

My nine-year-old son Aidan was carefully and slowly washing a peach in the sink. I was thirsty, and asked if it was ok if I filled my glass. He said "thank you," as I took the full glass to my lips.

I paused, and asked him why he thanked me, and he said,

"Thank you for treating yourself like you matter."

Time stopped for a moment as I took that in.

Days have passed and I still savor this idea and want to roll around in it and try it on from different perspectives. I decide I want to experiment with it. I realize that I can only really treat myself like I matter when I actually know who I am. I start to realize that I'm not just an isolated individual but part of a tapestry of love that is woven from every possible angle from every possible thing in the Universe, and the thought takes on another dimension. I treat myself like I matter when I come back to my heart and my breath instead of getting wrapped in drama or hooked by a false need for approval. I treat myself like I matter when I take the time to understand myself, to know what I want and how I feel and what I really think.

When I look at my life from the perspective that it is a living parable, rich with multiple layers of message and meaning, I begin to feel the magnitude of the gift that it is. I can almost hear the Beloved saying to each one of us, "I love you so much . . . I cannot tell you in words alone. I think it will take lifetimes to show you."

I am writing this book for myself and those I love, to bring my thinking about the past into clear definition to help me receive this life of mine as the gift it really is, to see the hidden meanings inside the parables so I can move into a place inside me that liberates, and live from that place. I am writing so I can learn how to love myself well and wisely, and create the conditions right here on Earth for the Home that I've been seeking for myself and my Beloveds. I spent a lot of my early life trying to get away, trying to leave by disassociation and by fantasizing about dying and suicide, from the mistaken belief that my Home is anywhere other than where I happen to be right now. This book is studying the art of knowing that I'm infinite at the same time that I dance, each day, with the reality that I am alive only for a short time: *what do I want to do with the time that I'm here?*

I want to learn who I am.

I want to share love.

I want to come Home, here, and be with you.

It is closer than we think, it is closer than thought.

I love you.

Pass it on.

Trina Brunk
9/5/2015

Prelude

Woman of Clay

Hers was a face upon which the strain of maintaining an outer appearance was beginning to show. It was in the smile that had lost its conviction but was still pinned up at the corners: hanging there, dangling in the wind, forgotten.   In her face you could see responses to all the concretionary shoulds, the sedimentary musts, the assorted conglomerate opinions that she'd become adept at collecting and responding to without even thinking.   It was an abstract skill, one that made her wary of encounters with two people of strongly differing interests while it simultaneously made her a little vain of an uncanny ability to gain instant approval in many social situations.

On the day of her twenty-seventh birthday, however, she drew herself up straight and looked down her nose at the train of events that had led her up to this point. "Today," she thought to herself, "I have had quite enough of this nonsense." She realized that she really didn't like the social situations she'd found approval in and that the musts and shoulds were crushing her and the opinions were becoming far too numerous and outrageous to properly catalogue and respond to.

"The first thing to go," she said, "is this smile." As she tugged a corner of it the rest of it fell easily away and she was left feeling the full weight of her substantial face. How tired she had been, and hadn't even known it! She allowed her feet and belly and whole body to sink into the earth, melting, dissolving, until they were shapeless, formless, a mass, and then as deep and as quiet, and then the same as, the earth itself.

Tattered nerves stopped trying to send and receive messages. They simply rested where they found themselves, mid-thought, mid-sensation. Rested.

Relentless cycles of obligation tooted their horns outside her window and waited. She did not emerge. One by one they slowly drifted away, one by one they left with their shiny "opportunity" blinking flashing light signs. Someone else would answer them.

And she rested.

Chapter 1

Coming home

I was the middle child of nine, born right after my only brother. I arrived six weeks ahead of schedule and spent the first two weeks of my life in an incubator, under bright lights and in a separate hospital from my mother. When we were finally reunited, she did her determined best to help me thrive, wearing me close in a pouch she made and nursing me. Under her care, in the face of the doctors' pessimism, thrive I did.

The home I grew up in was set in a beautiful valley amid rolling hills in rural Missouri, with a creek and forests and meadows where we would explore and play with crawdads and turtles and salamanders and toads. I remember getting up early and making my dew-drenched way down to the garden where Mom was working to the song of the bob white quail. Dad worked in a factory in the city while Mom and kids worked at home. We raised our own food in organic gardens and had goats and chickens and cows and a pony. For a time some of us kids, including me, were homeschooled. We sang together, my sisters and I, oh, we sang. Songs from Broadway musicals poured out of us while shelling beans and folding socks and cloth diapers. Mountains of dirty dishes transformed into a clean kitchen to Sinead O'Connor and Handel. Christmas carols sung in four-part harmony pierced cold winter air, offered to neighbors who in turn offered us cookies and glimpses into their holiday-bedecked living rooms.

My parents had a strong foundation of spiritual devotion set within their Primitive Baptist religious tradition, which strongly flavored their child-rearing and dominated our social sphere. My understanding of life rested comfortably in that place of sureness about the way the Universe worked.

Suddenly and uncomfortably, however, my perspective expanded during two early "awakening" experiences that radically shifted how I saw the world, and subsequently triggered a lifelong struggle to integrate what I'd experienced.

I was 14 when it first happened.

One early winter morning before sunrise I was drifting somewhere in the place between asleep and awake when I felt soothing, cool hands with long fingers gently lifting me up out of my bed, to a place that was awash in love. With a surge of joy, I recognized this place as my Home. There was a circle of many beings of pure light, and I was one of them. I felt so loved and so peaceful. I remember telepathically communicating with these beings. They were telling me something that I understood at the time, something that I was agreeing to, but couldn't quite remember afterward. Then with a "thud" I felt myself released back into my bed and into a life that was now split in two by what had happened.

Before my journey, I had not known anything different. Now, upon my return, I ached for more of that love, and I grieved.

At the time, I was a homeschooling teenager poised to enter public high school. Feeling socially awkward and with wobbly self-esteem, my main agenda had been to figure out how to blend in and appear "normal". I already felt like an alien. This cosmic experience did *not* help.

I did not tell anyone about this incident and it slipped into a hidden pocket of my mind. It didn't cross my mind until decades later.

Chapter 2

Born again, kind of

The summer I turned 19 brought another wake-up call.

I had followed my sister Toni to northern Alabama for a new adventure: a summer business internship program. The bulk of the job was selling Bibles and educational books door to door, and I was mediocre at this, at best.

As a child, part of our homeschooling had been to read the Bible aloud together, so I had a pretty good general knowledge of what was in there. As I grew, however, I developed an attitude of ambivalence toward all things Biblical, so it's funny that one of my first jobs was as a Bible salesperson.

My parents' religion was decidedly non-evangelical, and taught that Jesus had done all the hard part of saving people beforehand, so I was unprepared for the people I'd meet who would try to "save" me and wouldn't take no for an answer. I developed polite and evasive things to say, sometimes resorting to outright lying just to get out of a situation. Increasingly, the guilt was catching up with me. I hadn't been a good liar before and I'd have to become one if I was going to keep going down this path. I knew in my heart that I didn't want that. One evening, I cracked.

It had been a hard day. Slammed doors, dogs barking, hot sun, poverty like I'd never seen it before. I hid in my car alongside a dusty side road in the shadow of a cornfield, and I cried.

When the tears were done, I wiped my face dry and determined to knock on just one more door before calling it a day.

At the next house I came to, I was met with kind words and a glass of cool water. I started to show these folks my book samples and give them my sales speech, but they were actually interested in me as a person. Their kindness caught me off-guard, and exposed my vulnerability. This was their opening, and they grabbed it.

"Honey, have you been saved?"

I felt a troubled "No," coming out of my mouth before I could stop it, and could not hide my tears. Instantly they got their preacher on the phone and he came out and prayed over me, and I said the prescribed words and everyone was happy.

I was relieved to finally get into my car.

I had faked it, and I knew it.

On the way home I found myself apologizing to Jesus for my inauthenticity. What had happened in that house had felt forced. I didn't "know Jesus as my personal savior", no matter what I'd said. I realized suddenly that I wanted to know who he was, not from a book and not from someone else's ideas about him. Directly from him, and I said so, right from my heart to his.

No gentle hands this time. I don't remember how I got there but suddenly found myself amidst the rubble of a city in ruins, with smoke everywhere. I was desperately searching for someone. It might have been a family member. It might have been myself. I could not find who I was looking for. Then, to my horror I saw someone's arm sticking out from under a giant heap of smashed concrete slabs. Despair gripped me.

Then something inside of me started sounding, almost imperceptibly at first and then increasing in clarity. Something strangely and sweetly incongruent with everything around me: it was a Knowing, beyond words, that all was well. This Knowing kept humming, resonating inside my heart until it became more real than anything outside of me. The beauty of it lifted me up to the top of a mountain nearby. The city lay smoldering below, but I was safe and radiantly whole and peaceful. In a way I still find difficult to describe, I felt as though I was all of humanity even though I was in the form of one person. Arms upstretched, I was illuminated completely.

I don't remember how I ended up back in my car, parked on the side of the road under a waxing gibbous moon. This journey had fuzzier edges than the first one. But the impact remained for weeks.

I was God-drunk.

It was sweet but awkward to be in public with this feeling, like finding out that the boy in math class liked me as much as I liked him. At the next business meeting for all the interns, I found suddenly that all I wanted was to stand in prayer with others. Everything was lit up and prayers were nectar, bliss pouring through me as I drank in the light. Everything was bathed in the same luminescence that had filled me during my journey to the Mountaintop. I confided in my roommate, Patricia, and she nodded knowingly and congratulated me; apparently this experience was common among those who had been "saved".

Closer Than You Think

So this was what it was like, being saved. It was nice to have a category to file the experience into. But something didn't sit squarely. When I'd asked Jesus to tell me who he was, he didn't show up as a person, much less as a bearded man in robes. The only living person in the vision was . . . myself. And that certainly didn't compute.

I quickly distanced myself from that detail. I had an uncle who had suffered from mental illness and occasionally (sometimes violently) insisted that he was Jesus. He committed suicide and there was horror and grief as well as some relief at his passing. I hoped I wasn't going down the same route.

I wondered what was next. I didn't know how to carry this full-on bliss state; it seemed too conspicuously out of context with the rest of my life. The Light had planted itself in me, but it had not removed anything of my former awkward self. All of the old me was still there, and extremely uncomfortable with the situation.

The newly awakened light seemed to require something that I was unprepared to give: all of me.

I understood, rather than heard, an echo of the conversation I'd had with the light beings when I was 14. It was as if I'd agreed to let myself be consumed, transformed by loving light, and to radiate it on Earth.

But when I felt this brilliance encroaching on a core wound that lay hidden near the center of my psyche, I stiffened. I felt sure that some part of me was about to be eliminated. Panicked, I pulled myself back from the holy flame.

"I want to!" I said. "But I don't know how! I need skills! I need time!"

I felt the light recede from my vision. Had I failed? Had it left? Ashamed and bereft, I tried to call it back. I was no longer high, and the world seemed darker and emptier than before. I was sure I had cosmically screwed up.

Now, looking back over the years, I see that Love kept calling, and Love inside me kept answering.   Just not always in forms that I recognized.

Chapter 3

Split peace

I explored churches, looking for a place where I could be with others who also knew the radiance that had ravished me. I was baptized a couple of times in different settings and repeated the right words to see if there would be more fireworks. No luck.

And apparently being Born Again didn't automatically include conversion to a church. I enjoyed the feeling of belonging to a club and I got several dates, but the neat and tidy programs I encountered didn't seem to have much to do with my experience. Too many people were excluded by these religious frameworks. My experience had seemed to explode frameworks anyway.

The mystery inside me wasn't looking for comfortable belonging, it was looking for deeper awakening, deeper communion, deeper devotion. So I continued to look.

I cast the net wider. I challenged my strict Christian programming and over the years encountered elements of what I was seeking in other settings. Sitting in meditation, getting Reiki attunements out the wazoo, learning yogic breathing techniques, singing bhajans, receiving darshan with Amma, dancing the sacred Bulgarian circle dance Paneurhythmy in the early morning dew-drenched grass, all of these gave me for a moment what I was yearning for, and then ushered me onward.

My Jesus experience seemed out of context with the church folks I encountered, and a little awkward to explain to other people who had no similar personal experience. I met a mistrust of Christianity in many places. I really did not seem to fit in anywhere.

I wanted more of that bliss stuff.   Much as I tried to hold on to the "good" feelings, though, the feelings that I was taught were "ugly" persisted.

Despite the idyllic setting of my childhood, behind all the beauty we created together, depression and deep pain ran like a gash through both sides of my family line. Like all families, someone in generations back bore heartbreak and losses too great to recover from, and handed the pain that they couldn't figure out what to do with down to the next ones. This legacy continued and each generation added theirs until it became an indecipherable mess. I couldn't have put it into those words at the time. I didn't know why the pain was there, but I knew that there was a lot of it. The unspoken rule was to make sure that no one on the outside knew; all outsiders seemed to see was how amazing and beautiful and happy we were. And we could sing in four part harmony, which was wonderfully distracting.

I have no idea how effective the ruse was, but I think that the vigilant effort to look good on the outside and hide the pain was embedded in me and fused with my sense of identity. "Thou shalt think positive", and "Thou shalt not be ugly" seemed to be the 11th and 12th Commandments. Mom could scream at us in *that voice*, beside herself with rage and then the phone would ring, and all would be love and roses. I thought it was weird until I was an adult and saw myself doing the same thing with my kids. OK, I still thought it was weird, but I understood what it might have been like for Mom a little better.

This sharp split in persona from outer to inner manifested also between masculine and feminine, between teenager and adult, between humans and God and nature. Intimacy was only sexual and only properly occurred between husband and wife, with the brief exception of affectionate snuggles with babies. It was the correct order of things. These things were separate, very different, and must remain so.

I understand now that this position was radically disruptive to the essential nature of my being, but it formed the ground of assumptions I existed on so I could not see anything else.

Being one of the "Sensitive" ones, I felt the pain acutely and made myself heard, sometimes loudly, from a very young age. There weren't words for what I felt so it came out of me in art and music, and when that didn't relieve the pressure, I expressed it in various forms of incoherence. As a toddler and preschooler I was known for my raging temper and inconsolable crying spells. My parents and siblings did their best to respond, and along with the frustration, impatience and teasing I received, there were many large and small acts of compassion and attempts at understanding. But I didn't understand myself.

I was 10 when I first seriously contemplated suicide, and suicide urges were regular visitors as I grew up and moved through adulthood.

It probably didn't help that the religious tradition I grew up with emphasized that this is a world of woe, and that all the good stuff happens after we die. I am guessing this wasn't intended, but the message I took to heart was that it would be better to just get it all over with. There was an attitude of biding our time here until we were called Home to that happier place. At the same time, it was clear that everyone was doing whatever they needed to do to prolong their lives and avoid death. I didn't ponder this contradiction; it just sat there and contributed to my mental mud.

Serious splits in my psyche would manifest as different aspects of my own personality that were unaware of each other, each of them asserting themselves in different contexts, at the expense of my credibility. I was good at looking happy and functioning well, at least to those who were distracted with their own pain and thus not really looking. When I first had the experience of someone really seeing me, I felt pinned to the wall.

This happened during a couple of sessions with my mother's therapist, Dr. Paul Janeczek, when I was 15. His attention was positive, but in the face of his focused presence I felt suddenly and bitingly aware of what a fraud I was. We didn't take the work past this point, but the value was immeasurable. I don't think I would have known otherwise what a mess I was on the inside. Uncomfortable as it was, it was the mirror I needed and that awareness simmered for years until I began to find ways to access my wholeness. And when the Light came calling, it was no surprise that I held myself desperately separate even as I tried to answer.

As I tell my story I think it might be easy for some to interpret a lot of what I'm describing as a mess of psychiatric disorders. And what I start to think is that the way our society tends to see ourselves as separate from each other and nature and God(ddess, or whatever you like to call the Divine Mystery) is just another level of this state of incoherence, and that we can't wish it away or make it OK by ignoring it.

As years unfurl, the memories of my early encounters with the light are framed and again re-framed in the context of greater life experience, and I unpack new messages from the experiences all the time. I still don't think I understand them fully. But maybe the quest itself is the main point. Maybe the love that jolted me awake planted the seed of a multidimensional pathway that never ends but continues to bring me deeper into who I am. Day by day, step by step I walk, connecting with members of my tribe and at the same time becoming aware of and intimate with all of my fractured, scattered parts.

Chapter 4

Practice: Parts Dialogue

When I got my first job with medical benefits that covered psychological care, I picked out one of the psychologists from the list and faithfully set up and attended appointments. I patiently tried to explain to the man in the nice suit where I thought my distress rooted from but he couldn't seem to stay awake. I tried to be more interesting but it didn't help. After I'd exhausted the allowed number of visits he impatiently sent me to the drug counter for an antidepressant prescription. I walked away.

I decided that if I was going to find an answer for my suffering, I would have to take responsibility for my own process.

I wrote in a journal with an intent to understand myself better. I experimented with giving each disconnected part of me its own space to be heard. I would listen deeply to each voice, without shaming or blaming. I grounded myself in the commitment that I would do no harm to myself or others. When I did this, I found that the parts of me I had judged as "bad" and tried to distance myself from contained powerful information directly related to my desire for transformation and transcendence. It seemed that sustainable Evolution was not possible without equal Involution: I would find that when I would give neutral witness to myself, my fractured parts would re-integrate into a new and stronger me, and I would gradually find that the bliss and joy I yearned for would effortlessly bubble up inside me. When I accepted my grief and pain and rage and confusion and listened to them, like I would to a dear friend, I would learn astonishing and wonderful things about my own needs and desires and dreams.

I learned later that this practice was not first invented by me and that it had a name: "Parts Dialogue"[1].

In tweaking the Parts Dialogue practice a little, I began to discover that I could connect with and communicate with allies, both

---

[1] I developed this practice through journaling while I was in my early 20's, and then in my late 20's met Richard Ruster, a transpersonal psychologist in Boulder, Colorado who was leading groups and individuals in a process that was strikingly similar to my journaling method but much more sophisticated. I was stunned and excited to find that there were others who were following this practice and that it had a name. We became friends and community members and I continued to learn from him for years.

resources within me as well as diverse and expanded perspectives outside me to help balance out the intensity of the shadow: hidden and profound wisdom, deep love and practical support that was activated when I would focus my attention, and ask a question or express a need.   Ancestral voices made themselves known and helped me untangle and address the painful stuck places I had inherited from generations past. Spirit guides responded with inspiration for my writing projects and help for my relationship struggles. My own Higher Self helped me to understand increasingly more about why I was here, what activities and choices were consistent with my purpose and how I could live more deeply and fully the way I wanted to.

I joke about "talking with the voices in my head". But dialoguing with the different parts of me and the life all around me, I have come to believe, is not part of the pathology, it's a path home, and is just as sane and necessary as dialoguing with other people. If we want coherence, we must open our willingness to befriend and even fall in love with ourselves and each other and our world as we are, right now.

And then we can begin to see how this beautiful world is maybe not broken, and maybe neither are we.

Nowadays, interacting with inner guidance is a part of my daily flow. I ask Nature's opinion about what to put in the pasta salad or how to best structure a paragraph, and consult my Higher Self about where we might go on vacation or what the next evolution of my business might look like. I'll ask the Nature Spirit associated with the basil plant which leaves I may have and check in with my kids' angels when I feel stuck in a difficult parenting moment. For me, this way of living is interesting and outrageously fun. But it wasn't always this fluid or easy.

I grew up in a strict authoritarian household, and it took me a while to understand and accept that my guides were seeking not to boss me around, but to be my friend and work together as a team. I gradually unlearned my early training that good people always put others first and didn't pay attention to what they, themselves wanted.

A feature of this position was a tendency to push off responsibility for my decision-making by obsessively asking guidance for what I should do. When I wouldn't give myself space to wonder and explore what I thought or what I wanted, the information coming through would get all wonky. Sometimes I got the feeling that I was being teased or pranked. Some of the intelligences I worked with were truly funny and playful. Others would just go silent or communicate a sense of being troubled until I woke up and realized that I needed to step forward with more of myself, to exercise my free will and make my personal preferences and intentions known — both to myself and to the teams I worked with.

Bottom line, I learned that the role I was invited to step into was not to be a passive "hollow bamboo", or empty channel, but an active co-creator.

I invite you to explore this practice, and bring your creativity into it.

1. Identify, as closely as you can, what parts of you are active in a situation. If you're having a hard time disciplining yourself to stick to an exercise routine that you know you need, for example, the parts involved might be your inner child and your inner parent.

2. Identify any additional support that the process might need. In the example above, there may be a need for a wise elder for the child and the parent to consult with to help them break their polarization so they can work better together.

3. Give each voice a name that generally describes its role, get each voice on an imaginary conference call, or a place setting at your table, or a shell in a circle at the beach, and then listen to what each perspective has to say. Writing down the dialogue is highly recommended because it

helps to make the conversation more tangible and allows you to refer to it in the future.

ഇ൦ര

Some creative ways to use the Parts Dialogue practice for your empowerment and liberation

DEAR BELOVED CHILD
(A REPARENTING STRATEGY)

I have yet to meet a person that got exactly what they had wanted to get from their parents, whether it was greater freedom or more structure; more love or more space; whether their parents confided inappropriately in them or there was chronic disconnect, or both. Human parents these days seem to come with stuck places, as a rule, no matter how hard we try. And human children seem to come with deep needs to reach for greater expressions of wholeness than their parents can reasonably deliver. This doesn't have to be a problem, though. Now that you're grown, there's a version of your parents that lives inside of you. Sometimes they just repeat some of the more painful things your outer parents did when you were both in your awkward younger days, scolding and shaming and criticizing and abandoning. Your outer parents may have evolved, or they might not have; but this is irrelevant when it comes to your relationship with your Inner Parents, which is the relationship that actually matters most to us grownups. You have the ability to infuse your Inner Parents with all of the qualities you needed to receive, including the ability to say "I'm sorry" and to really pay attention to you and stand up for you. In this Parts Dialogue, write a letter to yourself from your Inner Parents. Give them space to tell you what you most need to hear. Go all out.

> *"Dear Beloved Child, I am so proud to call you my daughter (son). It thrills me to see you grow and explore your life. I know that I wasn't as available as you needed when you were small. You did not deserve to be hit or yelled at and I realize this now. You deserved so much more attention and kindness. I am so happy that you are choosing to give that to yourself."*

Then — and this step is more important than you might think — put it in a self-addressed, stamped envelope, and pop it in the mail.

I recently ran into a friend who had participated in a workshop a couple of years ago where I asked participants to follow this exercise.   He said he had done all the steps, except putting it in the mail. It went on top of the fridge, forgotten until he moved, then he found it again and mailed it.

When he received it in the mail, opened and read it, he said he cried. He could not believe how much he needed to read those words, at that moment. Perfection.

TO MY LOVE

If you are longing for intimate partnership and have yet to meet someone you'd like to partner with, it can be good to create some space in your heart and mind and life for your Beloved before they show up. In this Parts Dialogue, write a letter to him or her as if they are simply away on a trip, and tell them all that you'd like them to know. Alternatively, write a letter to yourself from them.

ANGEL BABY

I say that I have three children, but in actuality I have six: three on this side that I get to hold and care for and watch as they grow up; and three babies on the "other side" who I will never get to hold. The losses were invisible to most, but deeply painful to me. Some of us long for babies that never come; others of us have children who never quite made it to Earth, or their stay was nowhere near long enough for our aching hearts. Dialoguing with them via writing or in a meditation can sometimes help to bring the closure that is needed, or, if you're open-minded, it can help to open a connection that continues to grow in love.

Q AND A

There's another variation of the Parts Dialogue that I've found helpful in accessing my hidden wisdom.   This is in simple question and answer format, where I lay out my full question, confusion or puzzle that I am working on -- I describe where I feel tangled and uncertain, without trying to fix it or figure it out -- and then when I've fully expressed myself from that not-knowing perspective, I change hats and answer from the part of me that knows.   There's something about admitting that I don't know something that seems to activate a process of discovery in me.   When I'm overly identifying with the part of me that is in confusion and chaos, it is also helpful to remember that there is wisdom in me too, and that part is ready to help.   This format of the Parts Dialogue has been indispensable to me over the years and helps me show up as a strong and effective ally to myself, while giving myself space to be vulnerable and real.

For more ideas of how to use Parts Dialogues to deepen and add meaning to your journey, please see the "Decisions" and "Agreements" sections in Appendix A.

Please be gentle with yourself.

Closer Than You Think

Following a Parts Dialogue, we may have a variety of experiences including greater feelings of freedom; peace; heart-opening; joy; and love.   We may also find ourselves going through a transitional time of greater confusion and intense emotion that we don't know how to respond to or interpret.   It is essential that we be patient with ourselves and others during this time, knowing that it's sometimes not possible to immediately move gracefully with a surge of emotional information that we may have spent half a lifetime ignoring, rather than developing fluency with.   It takes time to develop skills and awareness and intimacy with ourselves, not to mention to make the lifestyle changes that will honor and support the new life that's making itself known inside us.

Fortunately, once we have taken the first step of unplugging our life force energy, we get more aliveness and authentic power to help us on our way.   It can be difficult at first, but immensely worth it to feel more awake and alive. And the time we take to develop the awareness and skills becomes a deeply meaningful and special time of learning how to truly love and take care of ourselves.

Chapter 5

Hitting the road

Early in 2014, I found my will to make things happen in my life draining away. Nothing I could do seemed to reignite it. I had released a new album, Songs of the Beloved, at the same time that I was growing out of my relationship with the lover I had been with for three years and had written many of the songs for. Singing the songs in public became half-hearted and difficult. All of my music suddenly felt unbearably stale and contrived to me. I was willing to show up but my voice left me right on stage. I couldn't fake it.

Predictably, money became scarce along with my loss of will and I was worried that I wouldn't be able to make my mortgage payments.

Around the same time I began to have dreams and visions of cataclysmic Earth changes. I looked around me and felt a clear sense that the Earth was past her carrying capacity of humans who were living unconsciously and out of balance with the rest of life. I wondered if the scary part of my Jesus vision was about to be manifested. Terror gripped me through the nights and wrenched my breath away. I worried about what would happen to my kids if I died and they didn't, and the world was in a wreck and I wasn't there to take care of them. I began researching primitive living skills and invited the kids to join me in learning how to make or find shelter, water, fire and food wherever we were. The activity gave me something to focus on and the kids liked it, but I was pretty sure that we couldn't gain the necessary skills in the amount of time we had to work with.

I was reluctant to talk with anyone else about my fears until I spoke with my friend Ashley. She is a kindred spirit with spot-on intuition who was there when the SoulPath work first emerged. She helped me refine and understand it better. I found out that she, too, had been receiving messages that felt like "get ready". But for what? She wondered if the visions of upheaval and massive change were just metaphors for what was happening in our lives, wake-up calls that couldn't be ignored.

This sounded right to me too but I wondered whether the two perspectives were mutually exclusive. I was finding it difficult to care about my own life as it was and couldn't figure out how to make any meaningful changes. The urge to give up was gnawing at me again. This time I decided to investigate it, and got out my journal and pen and opened a Parts Dialogue between my Suicide Urge, my Higher Self, Despair, and Me.

> Suicide Urge (SU): . . . . . . *Ache. No meaning. How much more time do we have left? What else do I have to do before I can go? Can I just grow a cancer and check out that way? How 'bout being hit by a semi?*
>
> Higher Self (HS): *You're always free to go. No guilt or blame. If it's what you really want, it can be arranged.*
>
> *Pause. The bluff has been called.*
>
> Me: *I don't want to leave the boys. I know it's not healthy to use them as my purpose for living. But it's not OK with me to step out of their lives when they're so little. I want to see to it that they're OK and grown up before I go. I love them so much. And this hurts a lot. Help.*
>
> SU: *Waiting till the boys grow up . . . that is a long time.*
>
> HS: *Just for the sake of fun, have you thought of how your life might look, if things were the way you wanted them to be? Do you have any personal desires? Things you want*

*for **you**? Have any un-lived life in you, any dreams you haven't yet acted on?*

SU: *(Weary pause) Well . . . .*

HS: *Lay it on me.*

SU: *Never mind. It's hopeless.*

HS: *Be as outrageous as you like.*

Me+SU (We're starting to merge into each other): *I know it's probably impractical.   And I probably don't have the skills or strength . . . I'm nowhere near strong enough.*

HS: *Yes?*

Me (SU isn't separate from me anymore.   She's now feeling discouraged and frustrated, but not talking about dying): *Ok. I've always wanted to live in a sustainable home. An earthship. Or a cob house. Or a house otherwise built in the most sustainable and appropriate way for where it was situated. But . . . .*

(Despair picks up the phone)

HS: *Yes?*

Despair: *I wouldn't enjoy it.*

HS: *Why?*

Despair: *Because it would be isolated and I'd be living all alone.   Or with people I didn't like.   Or people who were not honoring of the space. Or we wouldn't be able to afford it. Or we'd do it, and then realize it wasn't what we wanted after all.   Or we'd do it wrong.*

HS: *Oh.*

Me: *I'm stretching.   I'm having a hard time visualizing the whole picture. It keeps blipping out. Will you help me stabilize it?*

HS: *Yes.*

Me *(Feeling a surge of reassurance):* *OK. So this is what it might look like. . . . I'm living with a group of people I love, who love me.   On land that I feel deeply connected with.   We're consciously co-creating heaven on Earth with each other and Nature as an equal partner.   The children are able to play and do their work of growing into who they came here to be. They have a good future to look forward to. We are healing the wounds of our ancestors and living in a new way that honors the balance of life and is resilient in the face of the complexities of these times. I have meaningful work that I enjoy and am good at. We are prosperous financially and in all other ways. I am happy and excited about my life.*

Despair and SU have fallen into silence and are at peace. HS and Me merge and I/we smile.

ജ

This inner conversation was one of several over a few months that helped me to accept that my need for change wasn't going away and that I needed to take action. The awesome house in the wonderful neighborhood might have looked great on me. But it wasn't a fit for my Soul. I wasn't sure how to get started; the Others who would co-create such a vision with me hadn't shown up and I had only general ideas about where to settle. But eventually it became evident that I would just have to get moving, and trust that Spirit could guide something in motion better than a stationary object.

So in late April 2014 I began my journey when I took the first steps to radically downsize my lifestyle. Without long range plans for where we would go, I signed a paper agreeing to lease my house out for a full year. I sold and gave away whatever didn't elegantly fit inside my newly purchased 1993 RV, which we dubbed "Madre Tortuga", and moved myself and my three young sons out of our four-bedroom house.   I had never so much as ridden in a moving RV before, and now with the help of a caring friend I was (with shaky brand-new skills) driving and caring for a 27-foot-long motorhome, dealing with repair issues and handling the complicated logistics unique to these delightful creatures.

I was terrified.

And it was exactly what I needed.

But more about that later.

Chapter 6

Away

So I have this confession to make.

I used to avoid being around you because you had a lot of pain in your energy field. And I didn't want to feel that. I figured you were screwed up and I just hadn't found the people who weren't screwed up. So I hung out by myself, waiting for the time when I'd meet those people. Someone I could feel safe with.

And I journeyed.

By some miracle of grace, in a far distant land I did find some of those people. They were beautiful. They welcomed me in and I felt warmed and loved. And love was easy, and came with no great price. Just to be myself, to stand up tall, to sing my truth. It was heaven, for a little while.

I felt myself growing stronger and more confident, more real, less pretend. I was the Duckling No Longer Ugly.

And.

At some point I started to feel this itch inside me. Maybe I am a migratory bird and my internal programming predisposes me to fly back to where I began.   In any case, somehow my flight path took me directly

back
to
you.

And it does, it still freaks me out that you carry so much pain.   It makes me feel like I did in those moments when I was small and everyone around me was hurting, and no one was talking, much less singing.   Only screaming or frozen in silence.   No matter that I am now big and know I am a swan.   It still sends me curling up in a fetal position, life force squeezed out of me like a sponge, hovering over me nervously, wings beating against closed window glass.

And you are so used to the pain, you don't even notice it or realize that anything is wrong.   Or you do, and you just accept that this is the way things are.   How do you carry so many burdens not your own, and still know how to love?

You are my Own, I am sure of it.   I have seen your feathers gleaming white under the muck and the mud.

ℰᏆℭᏒ

Waking up to a bleary morning, gritty film over eyes making eyelids redundant.

Dull ache in the heart and agitation in the gut.

Maybe, maybe we are not getting out of here now, or ever.

Maybe there is no Other Place to go.

Maybe instead of getting out . . . . .

Something stubborn says, "Dive inside, find Home HERE, now, inside of me, instead of going away to find it elsewhere."

Mind spinning with that thought.

How. . . ? How will I do it?

Closer Than You Think

Disciplining my mind.   Uncurling the infant from her protected
repose, pulling the life force back into my body with a
snap.   Surveying the damage.

With jarring immediacy

I suddenly see

that the you I fled from

was really me.

Chapter 7

Come back

When I was 26, I discovered a shiny new skill called applied kinesiology[2] which allowed me to use my body as a bridge for a crystal clear dialogue with my different parts via yes and no questions. It was as if a hidden door in the universe had unexpectedly opened to me. It was then that I began having

---

[2] Applied Kinesiology: A technique of muscle strength testing used to help discern what affirms or strengthens the wellness of a person and what does not. It's that thing your chiropractor does when s/he asks you to hold out your arm and resist a pushing down motion to see what supplements are good for you or what food your body is having a reaction to. With a few extra steps, applied kinesiology can also be used as a strategy for accessing an expanded perspective, i.e. spiritual guidance, and in my case, allowed me to test the waters of refining my communication with Nature and more clearly discerning Nature's responses. To learn more, an online search will turn up many resources for learning how to use Applied Kinesiology for yourself. While it can be used to help expand your perspective, its accuracy is never 100% and is not to be used as a replacement for rational judgement or as a substitute for taking responsibility for your decisions. As the Bible verse (1 John 4:1) cautions, please "test the spirits" and use common sense.

conversations with Nature, a delightfully alive, joyful and wise part of me that I have come to love and respect deeply.

In these conversations I began the meticulous work of teasing apart the tangled strands of my emotional pain, asking and receiving extremely supportive information helping me clarify my feelings and thoughts.

In my family as I was growing up, until Mom started seeing Dr. Janeczek, there had been very little acknowledgement or awareness of emotions other than happiness or anger. Without support in understanding what happened inside of me, I experienced my inner life as an inarticulate, uncomfortable mess.

During my early experiments with kinesiology, I would ask Nature to help me name what, exactly, I was feeling: what it was called and what it told me about my needs. Somehow I trusted that if I could give myself space to feel uncomfortable emotions, they would eventually pass, and this was true for many of them. Some of them, however, persisted beyond all the attention I could give them. In some cases this was because the emotion was spurring me to take some self-care or integrity-based action and the feeling would not be resolved until I had done something appropriate. Some emotions stubbornly remained, however, and this was when I learned that a lot of the painful, persistent emotions I experienced were not my own. I learned that this was called being Empathic.

At first I considered being an Empath as a kind of a superpower: I was privy to the emotional secrets of others. Even though it was typically uncomfortable, it was a boost to my ego and made me feel special and superior.

The "gift" came with a price, though. Sometimes it made me physically ill. There were times when I would almost pass out or when the pain was such that I couldn't think clearly. My energy levels were often very low and my ability to function well was often seriously compromised. Large social gatherings were perfectly awful for me and I would dread facing the masses of people at my parents' home during holidays. I resented the painful intrusions and figured that my family was more screwed up than most.

Eventually I began to understand that my "superpower" was not just unique to me, but that the way I experienced so much of others' pain was both unhealthy and unhelpful. I realized, to the discomfort of my ego, that *everyone* has access to the emotional field, but that I would typically only feel others' stuff louder than my own when I was unconsciously disconnecting from myself in some area, typically mirroring what I was feeling from the other person.

I had hoped that I would learn how to use the emotional information I received to help others, but without being grounded in my own self, this sensitivity only alienated me from others and increased my frustration. My insistence that my ex-husband face his inner turmoil on my schedule rather than on his, for example, became a power struggle where my energy went to trying to figure out how he could feel better (so I could feel better), and his energy went to resisting my efforts to fix him. I decided that he just didn't want to grow and gave up on him. Now that we've been divorced for a number of years I can see that he grows just fine; he has his own pace and his own style that I can't take any credit for.

Slowly, reluctantly, I began to understand the heart of the issue: I was feeling others' emotions and needs before (or instead of) taking care of my own. Any claim to victimhood fell down in the face of the realization that I was creating the conditions for my own suffering, all the while contributing to the suffering of others. It took a while, because the victim mentality seemed to attract support, and I hadn't developed the skills or awareness for emotional self-responsibility yet.

But I was learning.

Using kinesiology, I asked for a clear message about what to do to take care of myself. I was urged to write a song.

But how? I had no idea. Songwriting seemed magical, something only special people could do. I figured that I needed some inspiration, so before I went to bed one night I asked for a song to come to me.

Early the next morning as I was riding the currents of sunlight into the new day, I heard repeated whispers, sweet words and melodies that I could only partially grasp, but that had me reaching, yearning for more.

I listened as long as I could keep still and then got a pen and paper and began writing, filled with exhilaration. The audible stream soon stopped, but I felt the words and music continue in the form of energy over the next few days. In this way I co-wrote my first song with Spirit and called it *Breathe In The World*. It contained all the seed thoughts I needed, and when I sang it, I was lifted up and filled with delight. It was contagious, too. I debuted the song at our local Unity church and to my amazement and sudden panic, received a standing ovation from the congregation of 200 people.

I continued to receive invitations to sing to this enthusiastic and loving group, and began singing to other congregations as well. Over four years I co-wrote nearly 60 songs with Spirit. Stage fright had me shaking so hard sometimes that I could hardly stand still, but as I learned to focus on my own ground, this eased considerably. I found myself enjoying the intensity and opening up to the flow of giving and receiving love in the form of music with the groups I would sing to.

Co-creating something of beauty with Spirit seemed to give me the bulk of what I needed to drive a wedge between me and my unhealthy empathic patterns. Putting on my songwriter's hat, I positioned myself in a place that had no room for victim stance. Together, Spirit and I turned the flow of energy around so that I experienced Source moving through me, giving no room for other people's unconscious distress in my inner space. And everyone seemed to feel fantastic! Wow!

Over the years, however, I occasionally felt stuck in situations where a song was not readily available. Sometimes I needed more mundane skills and awareness. For these situations, I was offered a simple but effective thought experiment that helped me sort myself out and come back to sanity.

Practice: Empath Self-Care

When I was ready to let go of the imaginary importance that being an empath gave me, Nature gave me a very simple process to disentangle myself from emotional enmeshment. It was these two questions:

1. What am I feeling?

2. What do I need?

I began to experience myself as stronger and clearer and more energized when I gradually increased my ability to stay with myself more consistently: to come back to my own heart, my own needs, my own intentions, my own emotions when I realized I had left.

And it continues. I used to think that Awakening was an event, something that happened and then you experienced freedom from then on. But for me, it is a practice of coming back, and back, and back.

I am still developing muscles around staying here at home with myself, still learning to see where I go unconscious, the blind spots where I might leave myself to escape pain or meet someone else's expectations or needs. Each place reveals more to me about myself, a precious nugget that helps me show up more fully and respectfully for myself and others.

Good thing there's music or it would get dreadfully tedious.

Chapter 8

(We are) the light at the end
of the tunnel vision

Around the time I started exploring with kinesiology, I asked
Nature the biggest Question I could formulate:

"What must I do to live sustainably on the Earth?"

Seemed like Nature would be the very best qualified consultant to
tell me how to do this.   Of course this was not a "yes or no"
question, and I scrambled to break down the topic into lists of
"yes/no" questions that I could test.   Where to start?   Paper or
plastic?   Go live on a commune? Become a bicycle commuter?
Become an environmental activist?   Become vegan? Where should
I live? How should I garden? How must I change?

Kinesiology's limits were immediately apparent as I felt caught in a scramble of mushy indecipherable non-answers.   My new feeling of juicy connection with Nature drained away.   Either my kinesiology was broken, or the answers were not accessible within my current framework of understanding, and I was clueless about what questions to ask in the first place. Which felt overwhelming and scary.   I set the question aside for the time being.

A couple of years later I was astonished and delighted to meet Rob, the first other person I had ever encountered who also practiced kinesiology and worked intuitively with spirit guides and Nature. We compared notes and discovered that we were both interested in sustainable living, Permaculture, unschooling, healthy living and intentional community. Getting married and moving forward on our dreams together seemed to be the most obvious thing to do, and six months within meeting, we married.

Our styles clashed immediately. I needed connection and intimacy and was ready for adventure, while he needed physical and emotional space and predictability. We did our best for eleven years. We lived in an intentional community with some beautiful souls who reminded me, by the love I felt with them, of the Light beings I had encountered when I was 14. I loved it and wanted to stay, but he was unable to find meaningful work that paid enough, and the idea of choosing differently from my spouse hadn't occurred to me yet. So we moved on. We had three beautiful sons together, all three of them home-birthed, and unschooled them. We moved to a nice house in a nice neighborhood. During the time we were together I started my design business and also began writing, recording and performing as a singer/songwriter.

Through all of this, we struggled. Our relationship dynamics continued to be painful and were becoming increasingly destructive when I decided to initiate the separation and divorce process. It was difficult but marked a turning point in our ability to function in a truly co-creative way. We continue to function pretty well as co-parents, much better than when we were trying so hard to make our lives and styles fit together.

In my 42nd year, 16 more years of expanding context and skills, I began receiving information that I gradually realized were answers to my Question along with greater understanding of why Nature's answers when I was 26 were so hard for me to grasp: it was because I was used to seeing things in parts, but Nature was re-training me to see in wholeness.

> Nature: There is so much to do here that you don't know
> where to focus.   You feel a bit scattered and it's well
> within reason to.   Resist the urge to stay locked in tunnel

vision; allow yourself to diverge from topic to topic; as your awareness rests on each area, you'll reveal a layer and address it.   You'll accomplish an amazing amount this way.   Tunnel vision comes from a belief that you should stick to something till it's done.   Reality is, nothing you focus on will ever be done; so flow with its continual evolution.   It's fun! This includes your work with your family and primary relationships, your growth and development, not just your quest for greater sustainability. It's all interconnected and you can't evolve the whole by fixating on the parts.   You're trying to "logic" your way through the transition but what is needed is for you to move and let your body teach you, to access your awareness beyond time and space.   Relax into trusting your connection with life.   There is nothing to figure out.

It's not a leap.   It's right where you are.   The path emerges the moment you walk it.   All you need is right here, right now.

Ցꝋ

Practice: Wide-Angle Vision

Will you try something?

If you're willing . . . .

Right now. Where you're sitting. Pick up a smart phone or computer or tablet and open an application you use frequently, and use it for a moment.   Check your email, go on the internet to one of your favorite sites. Text someone.

Now,

Notice how your body feels. How do your eyes feel? Your belly? Your throat?

Personally, when I'm looking at a screen, whether my smart phone or my computer screen or a TV, something happens in my body that is only OK if I can ignore it.   When I stop and pay attention, I notice that I'm holding my body in a tense pattern.   I feel tension in my belly, or my throat.   I might be slouching in a way that is actually uncomfortable.   If I pay attention long enough, my attention tells me I am not OK with the way I feel.   And unless I really Need to do Something with that device, I find that I prefer to put it down, to walk away.

What is it like for you?

If I still have your attention, I want to invite you to try something else.   After reading these instructions, put down your device and stretch your arms straight in front of you and put your hands together.   Look at your hands.   Now, arms still outstretched, slowly separate your hands out to your sides, and allow your vision to soften so it can expand to see your fingertips out to the sides.   See how far you can get your hands out to the sides while still being able to see them, wiggling your fingertips if necessary so you can expand your range.

From this position, I want you to notice how you feel.

Personally, when I move from tunnel vision into wide-angle vision[3], I find that my body opens up and I feel more alive and free.   Slowing down and opening my attention, I feel relaxed and in my heart.   I feel available to a flood of good-feeling life force

---

[3] Thanks to Jon Young and the Wilderness Awareness School for the name and inspiration for this exercise, which I've adapted.

energy. I experience myself as more connected with all that is.   It is really simple, but profound.   What do you experience?

Chapter 9

SoulPath Work

Nature explained to me that just as a sea snail knows how to build its perfect, spiraling shell, just as water molecules know how to come together in gorgeous snowflake patterns, our psyches and our communities also know how to be whole and in balance with the rest of life, and to create patterns with our lives that have beauty, symmetry and grace.

My work in understanding and integrating my inner parts gave me the context to begin to understand how I might view the world outside of me. I began to see how there is a way of being together that helps us to access and align with a Field of intelligence which holds the blueprint for our wholeness and connection. There are many names for this way of being together. Jesus spoke of it when he said, "Wherever two or more of you are gathered together in my name, I will be there with you." Among other disciplines, Bert Hellenger's Family Constellation work, John Upledger's

Closer Than You Think

CranioSacral work and Dr Usui's Reiki access this same Field from unique perspectives.   Artists and poets and musicians and other Mystics throughout the ages have intuitively known and been fed and taught by this Field.   There seems to be no one "right" way to express the wholeness, but rather, a diversity of perspectives brings more fullness to the Field.

Looking back over the years, I could see that at each step life gave me exactly the experiences I needed to shift my awareness so that I could begin to understand a little bit of what Nature was telling me in answer to my Question. Along with the Parts Dialogue practice, I discovered and developed processes, mini frameworks with which to map out smaller chunks of experience so they were easier to metabolize and integrate.   I tried on a few names for this growing body of work and SoulPath was the name that landed the most clearly.   I perceived that our Souls' path is not a straight line but a spiraling one; our way to making a Home here on Earth not a steep trajectory but a patient one that spans lifetimes and generations, while simultaneously bringing us instantly to exactly where we need to be. The processes and practices I was given seek to listen, perceive, and honor the Field, and in the process of being observed clearly, the Field becomes more clearly evident.   A quality of juiciness and peace and abundance prevails.   A feeling of deep connection and experiences of synchronicity are common.

Closer Than You Think

When we are operating in a way that is oblivious to the Field, in contrast, Nature showed me that humans create systems and patterns of dysfunction that travel way beyond our original (often well-intentioned) actions. The main areas where this disconnect manifests most tangibly and destructively are in the ways we collectively seek home, the ways we deal with death, our relationship with power, and in our addictions. Each of these four areas forms an axis on a matrix that holds our consensus reality in place. When we identify and release blocks to our awareness in these areas, the matrix changes and our lives change. It takes time and care and attention, and an attitude of humility and respect is essential. When we gradually begin to see lasting positive change at a core level, however, there is nothing more satisfying.

Please note: It is important to remember that the current state of the world didn't just happen suddenly; the distressing issues that we face on this planet as well as the beauty, love and wisdom we experience have been forming in our collective matrix for thousands of years and are the result of many generations' choices, conscious and unconscious. It's common and understandable for those of us who care about our planet and her people to feel an urgency to change things, hopefully for the better. Nature cautions us, however, against operating from the mindset of "push push push, hurry hurry hurry" which is actually at the root of many of the imbalances we've created. We are advised, instead, to

...sl o w d o w n...

. . . and notice how the quality of our consciousness creates the quality of our reality. The Soul's Path is epic in proportion; it unfolds over lifetimes and generations and eons. The transformations we seek are a relay, not a sprint (and probably not even a race); we are doing this together. The skills to cultivate are not self-denial and heroism, but depth of presence, patience, and staying connected in the face of suffering, in the face of accepting that we can't always make it better for those who suffer.

Here is another practice I was given. It utilizes the power of your imagination and your intuition rather than your logical mind to access relevant information that is held in the Field. It has the ability to help us bypass our ingrained mental patterns to take us right to the heart of what is going on as well as the next step in re-aligning with wholeness. You may do it by yourself, and you may also find it a lot of fun to do with friends. You are encouraged to use your creativity and modify the process as you feel moved to do so.

ΕΟΩ

SoulPath 101: The Basic Clearing

There is no reason you can't do this. There is no way you can make a mistake.   You may not necessarily do it exactly like I do; you have your unique way that is just right for you, so use my suggestions as a stepping-off point.   I dare you to go ahead and try it.   All that you have to lose is what holds you back!!

STEP ONE: SETUP

Have a pen and paper ready. Make sure you have some time in a place where you feel safe and that you'll be uninterrupted.

It is good to begin with a prayer for guidance or a statement of intent, or both.   Write down your statement of intent.

Journal Check in: How are you feeling? What is on your mind? What concerns have you had recently? What kinds of things are coming up in your life?   Are you creating something new that could use a clear landing pad to manifest on?   Where could you use some Divine assistance?

Ask for assistance from God/Goddess, your Higher Power, Jesus, or whomever you have an affinity for. Declare to yourself and them that you are ready for a shift, and willing to take whatever steps are necessary. If you're Atheist or Agnostic, you might choose to direct your declaration toward your inner mind. Whatever feels resonant for you is what is best.

Relax and allow yourself to be guide-able. In other words, admit to yourself that there are things you don't know and open your mind to the possibility of receiving a new perspective.

STEP TWO: GUIDED VISUALIZATION: ASK AND RECEIVE YOUR FIRST STAGE OF THE SESSION

Take a few deep breaths, and close your eyes, and allow relaxation to pour through you until it reaches every part of your body. Give yourself time to enjoy this sensation. Then, allow your mind's eye to imagine, see or sense a dial or a clock. Around the outside of this dial or clock there will be numbers, each number representing a stage of your life, past, present or future. When you can perceive this dial clearly, turn the dial until it wants to stop. Notice what number it wants to stop on.[4]

---

[4] Sometimes the dial goes right to a specific number, no ambiguity. Sometimes the dial stops at one number and then goes to another number. Sometimes it is blank. Sometimes it spins. Some people don't see a dial at all but see or hear a number, plain as day. I'm sure there are more variations I haven't seen yet. All of these variations can tell you something about what you're seeking to understand. Sometimes your imagination can give you information in a humorous way, using visual puns or other playful means. If you get stuck, writing down what you're observing can sometimes bring an "aha!" Also including others in this process can be extremely helpful, because your friends can often see for you what you can't see for yourself, and vice-versa.

This number represents a stage of your life.

A door opens in the face of the dial and you go through into that time in your life.   Look around.   Notice what is happening. Notice how you feel, who you are with, any words or phrases. Take your time in noticing all the nuances you can.

When you are ready, come back to the room. Notice your breathing, wiggle your fingers and toes.

STEP THREE: UNWRAPPING THE GIFT IN YOUR FIRST STAGE

Write down all you can remember of what you saw, felt and otherwise experienced.   As you write, know that each stage is archetypally rich with gifts that relate to the needs and/or desires that you articulated at the beginning of your session in the setup.

Generally speaking, in a beginner's session you'll find that the gifts that you receive will often fall into three general categories: Golden Moments, Limiting Beliefs and Frozen Feelings.

Golden Moments: These gifts are right on top.   Either your dial pointed you to a beautiful moment in your life that carries energy that you will want to bring into your present moment, or it carries a specific example of what you do NOT wish to bring into your present moment.   A reminder-warning.

Limiting Beliefs: Look for beliefs or conclusions about yourself, about life or about other people that were drawn based on your perception of the situation. These might be obvious or you might need to sleuth them out. It may be that something (good or bad) was true in that moment, and your imagination stopped there, and you have unconsciously limited your perceptions of all subsequent reality based on that one moment in time.   Or your dial may have shown you a place where a particular belief was in action already (not the moment of the belief's inception).   Important: these can be your beliefs or conclusions, or they can be those held by others you know, or those prevalent in a specific cultural mindset.   Check and be sure you've identified the relevant set of beliefs.   Once you've identified them as beliefs, there is no need to do anything other than notice.   The natural flow of your consciousness will do the rest.

Frozen Feelings: Look for places where your emotions felt too intense and you froze up, leaving a part of yourself behind. In these situations, imagine yourself sitting with the part of you that had frozen up in the face of an intense emotion, whether it was grief, terror, shame, regret or even joy or love.   Sit with the feeling, invite it in, breathe through it, allow it to flow.   Give presence to this part of you who didn't have the resources or strength to stay. Be with her or him. Gently coax her back into your body, if she is ready.   To the degree that you can do this, just breathe and stay in one place with your feet on the ground while feeling the emotion, you may find that you reclaim the life vitality and creativity of that earlier you.

There are many other kinds of gifts that have emerged in my work, but for the most part they are variations of the above themes.   I've included some of the ones I've discovered in the Appendix.   If you're willing and adventurous, you may find that you're discovering new gifts.   If so I'd love to hear from you about it.

After completing your first stage, check in with yourself and see whether you feel complete.   If you don't, repeat the process until you do.

STEP FOUR: TAKE ACTION

Review what you've discovered. Note any take-away's, any new awarenesses or things to pay attention to in your daily life.   Most importantly, choose an action step that will help anchor the shifts you made in your session.   The action step can be simple and ceremonial; it may be going ahead and doing that thing you've been procrastinating on; it may be connecting with someone, it may be adding (or subtracting) something to your daily routine.   Here is what I want to really communicate, though: No matter how exciting and wonderful your session is, *you only get to keep shifts that you take action on.*

STEP FIVE: GIVE THANKS.

Acknowledge the assistance you received and bring this experience of being supported into your daily life, knowing it is always there for you. Acknowledge with gratitude the elements of your journey, the difficult and the blissful, that made themselves known to you. Gratitude helps us integrate what we've received and primes us to receive more good.

ಸಂಥ

Tips for Excellent Sessions

A SoulPath session may feel wonderful; it may feel difficult.   Sometimes we are blessed with a sense of deep meaning; other times we're left scratching our heads, and we don't understand till later what the heck that was all about.   Don't try to force meaning that isn't readily apparent.   Just notice what you notice, and keep it simple.   Sometimes the meaning will come clear a day or week or month or even years later.

Staying grounded helps you to go deep and be more effective with the work.   It also helps the work to move more quickly.

Set a timer and take comfort breaks if the work is feeling heavy.   This is intended to be light work!   You may put the session on pause, take as many breaks as you need, come back when you're ready. But do come back.

Take care of your body.   Yoga, bodywork, walks in nature, Epsom salts baths, whatever feels like loving yourself is a good idea.

Be patient and gentle with yourself.   I have found that *"Infinite patience produces immediate results."* (Dr. Wayne Dyer)

Chapter 10

Food and ecstasy

Back to our RV journey.   We didn't go far; 40 miles west, to be
precise. The boys and I spent much of our summer at a farm that
was owned by a group of friends who had formed a small
community they called Green Dragon. Our RV was parked next
door to one of my dearest friends, Chris, and her family.   We were
on a beautiful Missouri hillside with lovely rolling hills and fields
and creeks and ponds. I got to begin writing my book, and as I
worked I could hear the farm's children and my children laughing
and playing with each other.   We pitched in and helped care for
the farm's animals and my boys were mentored by my friend Matt
in horseback riding, who along with practical help offered a good
balance of humor and a call to discipline.   That time was truly a
gift.   I got to deepen my friendships and my personal practice, and
I got to learn more about SoulPath work in practical application. I
was able to take off the mask and just be.   It also put me face to
face with my food.

Closer Than You Think

Today some guests visit the farm and we're enjoying showing them around. We stroll to the pigpen to empty out the compost into their eagerly snuffling snouts.

"Did you ever see an animal that looked more like . . . Bacon?" she grins. I smile with her. But I feel guilty of something, not quite sure what, until I take time to think about it later.

It's not that I think that it's wrong to eat meat.

But.

I notice that I stop shy of feeling into the Field around these animals. Different from cats or horses, whose emotional bodies feel noticeably familiar to me. I notice that I feel embarrassed at the pigs' eagerness to eat, and I remember feeling embarrassed for one of my sisters when we were kids and my dad insulted her, angrily called her a pig at the dinner table. It was dehumanizing and it stuck to her self-image like a flea on a dog.

I think about how ready we are to see horses as beautiful, but cows and pigs and chickens and sheep as utilitarian at best. I hold myself separate and superior from animals that I am willing to eat, and dive into exploring my connection with horses and deer and goats and birds.

Do I have to demean something to justify taking it into my body?

Does a life form have to be reduced in my regard to somehow being less than me, if I am to receive life force from it?

What if the life I take into my body is equal, or even excellently superior, and I am faced with that vulnerable moment knowing that I get to now stretch and yearn to be worthy of the Life that gave itself that I might live more abundantly?

What if it is all . . .

God
Giving God's body
so that God may awaken
in a new form.

What if it's all
Grace?
Take "Deserving" out of the equation.

It's all.
A Gift.

Closer Than You Think

Take it.
Give it joyfully.

I am what I eat.
Am I eating Grace with bliss and gratitude,
or projecting and then feeding upon projections, protections
against seeing, seeding the sacredness of life and the intimate
vulnerability that holds us all together?

What exactly am I eating?

When I feel that satisfying crunch and salty explosion in my mouth
am I massaging and placating that part of my Self that requires and
feeds upon explosive new discovery and learning and growth?

When I reach for that melting ecstasy of chocolate sweetness, am I
lulling back to sleep the intensity of my desire for ecstatic union?

Yesterday a carrot showed me how to die.

It was there in my hand, glowing, a ray of orange sunlight pulled
from the earth, scrubbed clean.   It had a funny twist in the middle,
like the center of a Mobius strip.

I asked it: *will you give me your body to sustain my body, your life*
force into my life force?

Closer Than You Think

And it answered *YES!!* with such a joyful rush
and with tears filling my eyes and my heart I ate.

And as I did I could feel that it was giving me something I needed
far more than physical nourishment, and that was this:
to know that there is no end. It is just life into life into life into life,
consciousness into consciousness into consciousness into
consciousness. Waves of never ending never beginning.

It's funny to me that we humans think we are the pinnacle of
creation, and it explains why we're so freaking terrified of
death.   If we're the pinnacle then from here, everything else is
downward. Maybe it would serve us to be a little less special. A
little less important.

Or maybe to see all the other places on the Mobius strip as
gorgeous as they really are.

*"Love says 'I am everything.' Wisdom says 'I am nothing.' Between
the two, my life flows."*

~ Sri Nisargadatta Maharaj

Chapter 11

Training

Somewhere beginning in 2014 Nature told me I needed training to help me ground and expand my process. I agreed and mulled over what kind of training would best position me to reach these goals. I researched some options I found online. Life Coaching or Counseling seemed right on, but as a working single homeschooling mom with scattered attention and few financial resources, I just could not conceive of how I was going to accomplish this. I set it aside.

After the boys and I got settled at Green Dragon, Nature brought up the topic again. With all the unknowns in my life it seemed more preposterous than ever, until I had a sudden idea.

"Nature, will you be my teacher?"

"I was hoping you would ask." was the response.

Chapter 12

Day 1

Me: *How shall I proceed?*

Nature: *By making a declaration of your hopes, dreams, intent.*

Me: *OK. I've been working on this but still feel kind of awkward, concerned I'll get it wrong and be stuck with the consequences of bad choosing. Still, I'll give it a shot because I think I understand that if I need to I can always revise my declaration.*

Nature: *That's right.*

Me: *I would like to live a life that moves ever more deeply into pure love. I would like to explore and develop my own co-creative relationship with you. I would like to learn how to easily manifest rich abundance. I'd like to channel that abundance into supporting a shift to regenerative lifestyles for humans on Earth. I'd like to be part of a group of close friends who are making a lifestyle together of love and co-creativity, honoring autonomy and enjoying resonance and beauty together.*

Nature: *Good. Come back first thing tomorrow morning before the boys wake up. Have a pen and journal and be ready to take down notes.*

Chapter 13

Day 2

Me: *Good morning! What are we to do today?*

Nature: *Work on the Trust Factor.*

Me: *Okay.*

Nature: *I'm not here to take over your life. That life belongs to the Infinite Eternal Source.*

Me: *I feel a surge of fear and disconnect.*

Nature: *Trace it.*

I did a SoulPath session and this is what I found:

I'm 13. It's January. Not much happening so I'm paying attention in church. They're talking about how the Devil is sneaky and will deceive you. I doubt this but the fear is planted. Afterward, the mistrust sets me off balance. How can a person know when they're being deceived?

Dogmatically positioned beliefs: You can't trust. You're not safe. Faithful Christians should only talk to God.

These under-thoughts were not what I would have consciously chosen, but they were persistently there and resulted in mental rigidity and fear of expanding beyond the familiar. I realized that I had kept my relationship with Nature at arms-length, always at a safe distance and usually just theoretical or pertaining to my subjective truth. Laying the beliefs out there in the open allowed me to review them and see where indeed I had fearful adhesions in these spots where I would hit a bump and reject our connection.

> Me: *I'm feeling the stuck places, not making them go, but simultaneously feeling new conscious awareness rise up and stir some things awake inside me.*

> Nature: *That is how SoulPath makes changes. Don't force the change. Let it come as it will, and it will be sustainable.*

Chapter 14

Day 3

On the third day, the question and answer journaling format shifted to a combined Me and Nature voice.

They say that power corrupts, and that absolute power corrupts absolutely. I think this is a mistaken and disempowering premise that leads good people to dodge the real work of coming into their authentic creative power and personal sovereignty, which is what makes them available to co-create in the first place.

I would start with a different premise, and that is this: that Power-Over is a way of operating that is based in flawed thinking and has catastrophic consequences for all involved. Power-With is as constructive as Power-Over is destructive.

Power-Over blinds us to our origins, our connections with all of life. Power-With requires more time, creativity and imagination, which is how Power-Over often justifies its means. But as is the case with increasingly fast Internet and device speeds, even with its demands fulfilled, Power-Over doesn't ever seem to be satisfied but instead seems increasingly tense, upset and frustrated.

When I look at the Judeo-Christian origin myth with its fall from grace, it casts God in the role of punishing judge, and I wonder if the original sin was this perceptual shift from being One with God and creation, to the illusion of separation. I wonder if this story represents our decision to enter the Matrix, experiencing reality through the binary state of Good vs. Evil.

Why did we want this? Why couldn't we be happy with hanging out with God in the Garden all our days? Were we really deceived? Was there a purpose to this wild and often painful journey we've been on since?

I like to think of this "fall" as the ultimate Soul Contract[5]: the beginning of an epic mythic Hero's Quest to ensoul ever greater aspects of the Universe, to expand conscious

---

[5] Soul Contracts are discussed in Appendix 1: Gifts.

*awareness beyond where it has gone before. This, I
believe, is the Soul's purpose for trauma.*

Chapter 15

Day 4

I had neglected to put up the RV awning the night before. The weather had been clear and pleasant when we went to sleep, but we were awakened suddenly by a huge crash of thunder followed by high winds and torrential rains and hail. I could hear the awning clanking and whipping around in the gale. Nature told me that it was OK in the storm and didn't need to be secured. I weighed my options. I could disregard this input and take care of the awning, which would have been the sensible thing to do. Or I could test it. If the awning broke, I could set aside this Nature thing once and for all as simply an interesting figment of my imagination. Because my sanity was on the line, which was more important to me than the awning, I decided to ride it out and see, even though I was terrified. (It could be argued that this was a sign of insanity, but let's take that conversation elsewhere.)

The next day broke drizzly but calm. We learned that there had been a super high-speed blast of wind nearby that snapped off large old oak trees like toothpicks and uprooted many more. But the awning looked to be OK.

Nature: *See? Now do you believe me?*

Me: *I think we're good, AND I will need to test the awning to be sure once the kids are awake. It's funny, because I've been having conversations with you for years. But. Yes. This trust thing is the next step. I'd say tentatively that we're good to continue. What is next?*

Nature: *Notice that you believe you don't have a right to test out your beliefs.*

Me: *Yes. I feel guilty and sure you'll be mad at me if I continue to question.*

Nature: *But that's what we need to build this relationship. Question as long as you question. Trust when you trust. Ask me for things. See what happens.*

Me: *OK. Aidan and Ethan had sunburns yesterday. Can you heal that? Will you?*

Nature: *Notice the fun and freedom you experienced when you enjoyed late night at the creek under the moon with them. If that's not healing, what is?*

Me: *Are you dodging my request? . . . OK, I feel a fullness in my heart. Gladness, love. I saw love between the boys. They were patient and they cooperated. We had fun. I'm feeling kindness, gratitude. Abundance of time for each child, fun to be had with each of them. And freedom for me when I let them be free. It felt gooood.*

Nature: *THAT is the state within you that evokes the healing response. It IS gooood.*

Me: *OK. (smiling) I do have a question about money. I need to learn to manifest money effortlessly, I think. That is my objective, right?*

Nature: *It's who you are.*

Me: *What do you mean by that?*

Nature: *When you're not fighting giving and receiving, you'll find that money wants to come to you. You can live wherever you like. You can manifest sweetness of home abundantly. It's right there for you.*

Me: *Another manifestation question. Tami (my astrologer sister) told me that my ideal partner is Capricorn. Someone to help me manifest my dreams, someone practical and supportive, who is eager to help me. I think that is you, am I correct?*

Nature: *Yes, that is correct. I'm here when you need me.*

Me: *Who, exactly, are you? I call you Nature, is that enough? You seem to have a personality. In my inner space you feel somehow luminous.*

Nature: *I take on a personality as necessary to connect with different needs. I'm actually personality neutral. You can think of me as Nature's response to your need for partnership right now. I can be your lover, guide, friend, teacher, provider, protector.*

Me: *Whew. That is huge.*

Nature: *Yes. And there is more, as needed.*

Me: *Women have tried to be this for men, and men for women. In my experience it's always ended up feeling like an entangled, self-abusive mess. And you're offering all this for me, in exchange for what?*

Nature: *I want to see the gifts we've manifested together so far reach a wider audience. Yes, the music, the SoulPath work, your writing. Your children. They are extraordinary individuals. I want to partner with you so that all of this, all of **our** children can flourish.*

Me: *OK. I accept. And I feel that twinge of fear from my religious upbringing.*

Nature. *It will be an ongoing project. Never worry that you can't afford to feel it.*

Me: *What is my part, again?*

Nature: *Ask for what you want and need. You may need to clear blocks and you may have to take "no" for an answer while something better manifests. But slow down. Live a life of beauty. Enjoy your kids. They are wonderful.*

Me: *All right. Thank you!*

Chapter 16

Re-stating it seems necessary

Nature: *Ready to try something?*

Me: *Sure, I'm game.*

Nature: *Here's the process.   First, Ask. Then, Clear. Then, Receive.*

Me: *OK, I'm taking notes. Then what?*

Nature: *That's it. You wanted more to do?*

Me: *Ummmm . . . I'm not sure this will work.*

Nature: *Try me.*

Chapter 17

The ticking gifts inside

getting ready to detonate

My training sessions with Nature continued through the summer in short but potent journal conversations each morning.

During this time, I was noticing how on the farm there was sometimes friction and patterns of disconnect between certain individuals. At first I felt depressed and discouraged by this. I wanted a more juicy love field to play in where everyone was seen and loved for who they were. I disengaged from colluding with their stories by becoming the person who stubbornly saw something good about a person who was being criticized or complained about. Fortunately my friends were patient with me. Someone commented that I seemed to have a talent for seeing the gifts in others. I liked that and decided to develop it more, and as I did, I started to have a whole lot more fun.

One of the ideas that I began to explore was that each one of us has a unique radiance, a natural way of being that is essentially good. It doesn't have to be taught to us, but it needs to be seen and it needs certain conditions to develop.

I started to experiment and look deeper at what each person in a conflict was really wanting and needing and what gift or quality was being overlooked. As I looked more deeply, I began to experience true pleasure in receiving my friends in a way that I hadn't before. Suddenly their struggles receded in my vision and all I could see was their light, and it was beautiful.

Here is what I began to believe.

∽◯∾

Our unique light, our true gifts, burn from the inside until we release them.

We can't go un-numb without feeling this.

Most of us, I'm told by Nature, have no idea what our true gifts are. Because we are unique, it sometimes happens that no one

— not even ourselves — recognizes our gifts and they fly past radar screens undetected. Sometimes they take forms that are socially invisible or discouraged, and it takes rare courage and vision to bust through that. Even if the environment isn't hostile, few of us receive adequate training to develop and become skilled at what we came here for.

I have a working premise that if we can uncover and activate them, the unique gifts within us are our answers to our current planetary crisis.   Is that far-fetched? I'm willing to test it out and see, because I can't think of a better choice.

In that direction, I am fidgeting and twisting and scraping off the old skin -- shedding the not-gift behaviors that I became skilled at because they garnered attention and approval and paid well.   I'm dropping the ones I developed as a rigid defense against the hurt of not being seen or heard or truly known — not even by myself.   And I am re-focusing my own attention on understanding who I am, and developing what it is I really came here for.

For me, being sensitive was a huge liability in a family where toughness and the ability to push past pain with a happy face were valued. I had no idea that sensitivity could prove to be a gift. When I started to learn about the Field and understand how it becomes stronger and juicier when we pay attention to the subtle nuances, I started to cherish my ability to feel deeply and value it as a pathway to learning more about Life and myself and others.

When we approach unwrapping our gifts questions often arise.   What if I invest myself in giving my gifts and no one wants them?   What if I can't figure out how to make it work financially?

And then there is the (sometimes justifiable) fear that our gifts are disruptive in nature, that they will bring us unwanted attention, or have a negative impact on others.

This is justifiable because our gifts carry so much power that they are indeed capable of disrupting life as we know it, and they will do a thorough job of it if we are acting unconsciously, or if our life as it currently is set up is oppressive to our spirits.

I know a man who has a profound gift of truth-telling. He doesn't intentionally set out to wake people up. It's just a natural expression of who he is. He opens his mouth and the missing ingredient topples out. When you're living with people who are reasonably awake and have done their work to disarm their defenses, such a gift can be celebrated and deeply appreciated. Not everyone is ready for such potent stuff, though, and as my friend grew up he encountered something less than enthusiasm for his sacred gift. Drama-filled and unsatisfying relationships resulted from his attempts to change himself and others. When he just let himself be, this opened up the space for something new.

Our gifts will change everything that needs to change, hurtling us into the unknown. If we've been in denial, this terrifies us.

What we don't see unless we take the step to uncover our unique superpower is that our gifts carry the seeds of new beginning in them, too. I feel this in my bones: we don't just get stranded. Granted, we may be living moment to moment, being spoon-fed babies in a new reality, but if we're willing to leave behind the places we had mastery, to reach out and become students of the Life within us ... each step of the way we are supported if we keep on breathing, asking for what we need, opening and receiving ...

And the only. Way. I know how to do this in any consistent way, is in the context of our soul's community. It's where our gifts have relevance and are seen and received. Where we seemed to be "too much" for our family or community of origin, our tribe depends on us showing up as fully as we can.

Soul friends are those people who understand what you're going through because they have walked that road or are walking it right now beside you. When you're around them you feel beautiful just the way you are. They are those people who weep with gratitude when you simply tell your truth, because it is true for them too and they didn't completely know it till you spoke it. They get to be more them, and you get to be more you when you are together. Their presence warms and strengthens us at points on the trail that would otherwise be too hard to bear.

If you haven't found your tribe yet, I ask you to take heart. If you are doing your inner work, if you are noticing what lights you up and if you are acting on your delight, if you are saying "no" to things that don't serve you, you are setting yourself up to bump into one or more precious soul friends. Doing these things prepares the space that will welcome and affirm them when they do appear, and it makes your life so much more lovely regardless. How bout it?

In the meantime, there are things you can do to quicken your connections with those you are with right now. For one, if you are in any proximity to a group of people that practices peer-based counseling, I encourage you to check them out and see if you resonate with their practices. Also, some of my friends have found exactly the kind of support they needed in 12-Step groups or in other support groups that form around the desire to grow and heal. There are others who have the same needs and the chances are good that someone else has paved the way, and that your participation will be welcome and nourishing to all.

One way you may find or build your tribe is in the shape of a circle. I am finding that the structure of a Circle, when approached with respect, tends to support us in staying aware of our self-responsibility and gives us perspective of ourselves and each other that can help us feel simultaneously more free to be ourselves and bonded with each other.   When I sat in council meetings in an intentional community, when I learned the sacred Bulgarian circle dance Paneurhythmy, when I visited the Pueblos and learned of the Kiva, I understood that I'm not the first one to make the observation that we find ourselves whole together in the Circle.

In my current life the Circle is coming alive in different forms too.   I went square dancing for the first time in years and felt so alive and free!   It's not actually a square; it's a kaleidoscopic moving mandala of many shapes, including a circle.   A dear soul sister has recently been calling together intimate song circles around a fire in her backyard.   Friends are playing music together and enjoying the sweetness of life, meeting new friends, circles expanding into other circles and connecting on and on. I'm so grateful to find that my need for my tribe is being filled often in ways that surprise me and pop me out of my set ways of thinking, and call me back to my unique gifts that must come awake in me, if I am to truly live.

ဆာ

Practice: SoulPath Circle

The SoulPath Circle is identical to the SoulPath Clearing, except you're doing it with one or more other people instead of by yourself.

You may proceed by reading and following the instructions together, or you may choose to have one person act as a facilitator. After the guided visualization is complete, each person takes a turn sharing what they experienced. The group can work together to understand the gifts that are coming through for each individual. Try to resist the temptation to over-think but rather relax and listen as deeply as you can. Stay in your own experience and speak from the heart. Notice any feelings you have as you listen to each other, whether resonance and excitement or tension or grief or frustration, for example. It's important to remember that your feelings and insights are firstly about you; understand that projection is an extremely slippery phenomenon, so anything you offer must be in a spirit of humility and respect. Report what you are personally experiencing and check to see if anyone else is feeling something similar or related. I find that people who never thought of themselves as particularly intuitive suddenly realize that their intuition has been strong and reliable their whole lives, and that this process helps them discern which voices are intuition and which are busy mind chatter or cultural programming. It is often amazing to witness connections that we didn't know were there, in relationships with those we are close to as well as those we are meeting for the first time. The gifts that emerge in the context of these circles can catapult everyone involved into a new paradigm.

Chapter 18

A message from home

Amidst all the beauty, I still experienced depression and loneliness. There were a lot of experiences I had that I did not know how to share with anyone else, and this felt isolating to me. I felt weary and older than 43. I wished for intimate partnership but was disinterested in the dating scene. Some days I felt like giving up. A part of me was still longing to go back to my origins.

Lying in my comfy RV bed one summer night I realized I was receiving a message from an unusual source. It did not feel like the touch of Nature in my mind and I cast about trying to identify who it was. The feeling was sweet and ethereal and oh, so loving and sparkling and filled with beauty. I realized with a start that it was the Ones who had awakened me that winter night back when I was 14. I began to weep.

"You've come back! Thank you! I need your help!"

Confusion registered on the other end of the connection.

Suddenly I realized that they were telling me, in their nonverbal way, that they hadn't come back to help *me*; they were requesting *my* help.

And the whole paradigm shifted.

I suddenly saw that my perception of my own neediness was an error, a baby wishing to go back into my mother's womb instead of facing life. I had all of that light and love inside of me, and my job was not to figure out how to get back where I was before and bask in safety and security with them, but to take the beauty and spread it, share it as far and as wide into the universe so that no matter what happened to them, or to me, our love would always live on somewhere.

"I will do my best," I promised.

Chapter 19

Power imbalances: a shift in perspective

On August 9, about 140 miles east of where my RV was peacefully parked, a young black man named Michael Brown was shot to death by a police officer. His body was left lying on the pavement for four hours. This was not, unfortunately, as unusual as it was horrible. What was unusual was that the incident was not successfully brushed under the rug. Instead, the authorities' refusal to properly investigate and the police's military-scale retaliation to mostly peaceful protests ignited the fuel of years of oppression in cities all over the country, and got the world's attention.

I was struggling with a thought which Nature had offered me: that power imbalances are illusions based on a mutual agreement to see, value and honor only one form of power[6]. When the party

---

[6] See Appendix: Power Imbalances

that experiences disempowerment learns to see, value and leverage the power that they have, the experience of "imbalance" dissolves. I was particularly feeling disturbed at the assertion that oppressive power structures could be effectively dealt with just by a shift in perception on the part of the oppressed. It sounded like magical thinking. I fantasized about these power structures, multinational pharmaceutical companies and corrupt governments and for-profit prisons and the like, collapsing from some miracle of Grace, because I really couldn't see any other way for things to be set right.

> Nature: *You are waiting for God to come in and rescue you from these Others who are in domination mode. But what you forget is that YOU were given the same power as these Others. That is the crux of the matter. The domination game is to distract you, point you away from your real power, to lead you to believe that you are powerless, wounded, confused, and so on.*
>
> *It's all a lie.*
>
> *Oppression works as long as you believe that it is possible for you, a brilliant eternal Creator Being, to be oppressed. As long as you believe that you are separate from your Source, you will be at war with yourself and with the*

Other.   The moment you recognize the lie at the heart of this and restore your awareness that you were made perfect in every way, the truth of the Universe is restored, and you are free.

Me: *Ohhhkkkkaaaaaayyyyyy . . . .*

Nature: *Yes?*

Me: *Well.   Right now, at this moment in Ferguson, Missouri, there are people who are being tear-gassed and treated like the Enemy, just for exercising their right to protest murder, blatant racism and abuse of power.   What would you tell these people right now?   That they just forgot, to get all peaceful and remember they are One with Source?!! They're getting pummeled.*

Nature: *They're getting opportunities to connect with the power inside them.   And many of them are doing it, waking up and joining together in ways that will last long after the smoke clears. And in the process, the world watches and many others will become awake.   It's time. The more people wake up, the more miracles of solidarity and love and courage you will see.   Many will be hidden from your view, but know they are there.   And know that they are inside of you.*

Chapter 20

Love and liberation

October in Missouri is typically gorgeous, with just enough chill in the night air to urge readiness for the cold weather. During that window, I chose to move myself and the boys out of the RV and rented a house in town for the winter. During the tumble of this transition I also fell in love with D__, a man who lived far away from me. In our telephone conversations the energy was strong between us and the connection warmed me in places I had forgotten were there. I got to explore the edges of my own psyche in this place called "falling in love" and had tons of really wonderful conversations with Nature that helped me integrate the intensity and have fun in the process.

ഇⓒൻ

Nature: *This stuff about sex and attraction is key to your work here on Earth, so listen up close.*

You can't get what you think you want from someone who doesn't have it to begin with.   Even if they supply what you think you want, you'll be disappointed to find that the target has moved somewhere else.   There is no way to prevent this from happening.   What you seek lies elsewhere.

Me: *It's hitting me that I've spent most of my teenage and adult life feeling obsessed with getting into a relationship, or out of one.   Persistent nagging thoughts of the other, trying to catch someone's attention or trying to keep it, trying to present myself in a way that would wow him again like I did that one time, phew.   It's pathetic.   I know it.   Why is it so hard to stay grounded and real around relationships, sex and all that?*

Nature: *You left a part of yourself back there and you're trying to get it back.   Most relationships are about trying to recover something you perceive to be missing in yourself from the other person. But it is usually so unconscious that you don't recognize the fact until some time later, if at all. That is why people often become so entangled with mates they don't really understand or even like. So many people just tolerate each other, but can't seem to improve the dynamic, and either dig in and stay for the long bitter haul or leave the relationship, only to repeat the cycle somewhere else. But when you access the Oneness inside of yourself, sex becomes about so much more. It becomes an opportunity to discover something deeper, to liberate greater awareness. Your vulnerability and willingness to be open and share and love is wonderful for your partner, of course, but even more importantly it is a gift you give your own self.*

Me: *It's embarrassing to me that I have such a one-track mind sometimes. Why do my thoughts go to sex and partnership so compulsively?*

Nature: *First, understand that any obsessive thoughts are you, trying to distract yourself from something else. Obsession about another person (or anything else, for that matter) has nothing to do with the other person and is the addictive mind's attempt to keep you from dealing with a core issue.   Usually you're unconsciously trying to shield yourself from your vulnerability or aliveness, both of which are perpetual states that you have no control over.   When you enter into an intimate partnership, your awareness of your vulnerability and your aliveness are amplified. This is exciting . . . and it's also dangerous to your ego. You shift unconsciously into trying to control how the other person perceives you almost immediately by making sure you look good. How you look, act, dress; what you drive, how financially successful you can appear to be. Courting becomes not an invitation to get to know each other and have fun, but an attempt to covertly get something from the other person without giving away your real coordinates.   It's a trap.*

"Turned On" is your natural state when you're plugged into your life purpose, feeling Source flood through you, and you opening in response.   When you feel it in relation to another person, this means the other person is reflecting back an aspect of your wholeness that you yearn to re-integrate.

Being turned on is YOURS.   That other lovely person is just a reminder. Enjoy!!

Me: *Why is it such a turn-on to think of someone as being my life mate, the One for me, and a turnoff to think of someone I'm with as being a temporary partner?*

Nature: *It's understandable that you're looking for someone to be the One.*

Your mistake is that you're trying to find that One in someone else, when the One you are longing for is actually your Self, whole and healed and fully alive, awake and aware. You project your needs, your longings and hopes and dreams and desires on this Other, and then when they show up positively, you compulsively try to devour them, and you call this love. When they show up in a way that doesn't match your ideal, you freak out and start to act nasty.

This is a feverish dream.

Wake up! Your "passion", your "attraction", isn't about the other person. It's about you.

Me: *I recognize truth in what you're saying, but feel worried that you're telling me that my quest for loving someone and being loved is based on illusion.*

Nature: *Loving and being loved is very real and very powerful. The popular saying that you must love yourself before you love anyone else is a start; I would amend it to say that the moment you love yourself, you love others. It's not either/or and it's not bound in time or space. It's both/and, and it's simultaneous. When you believe you love someone else and you don't care for yourself, look out. Your lack of self-love is the hidden agenda and it must be addressed if you want true love. And if you truly love yourself, you'll find love everywhere. This doesn't mean that you partner indiscriminately, but that your core needs for connection and learning and growth are constantly being fed.*

ℰℭ

TO MY LOVE

Sometimes the resonance between us hums so strongly I feel sure that I could reach through it and touch the face of God.

Sweet mask to my mask of the Beloved, when this form falls away will we be caught naked and giggling in the full light of awareness Knowing that there only has ever been Lover and Beloved?

Dripping heavy laden with love stuff
I gasp in the sudden pleasure of taking this truth into my hidden
darkness:
that I am part of you and you are part of me.

Miles away, you think of me and I am with you.
Though unseen, I reach out and touch your skin.
Futile longing expands separation to infinity;

Simple acceptance, and you are here,
with me,
breathing the same love fragrance.

Practice: Intimate Partnership Re-Calibration

Sometimes it can seem that the relationships we call "love" relationships can get so tangled, and about anything except love. This practice helps us gently untangle and disengage from unnecessary drama, and re-focus our energies in the direction of creating what it is that we desire. Whether it's the blissful sweetness of Divine Union, expressed in the physical, or soul-satisfying friendships, or mutually beneficial co-creative partnerships, so much is available to us. I want so much more for us than what we often give ourselves. Here is one way to claim it.

STEP 1: CONCERNS

Write through all that concerns you about your partner.   All of it.   Don't sugar-coat it.   If you have a tendency to pull the wool over your own eyes in order to protect yummy feelings from evaporating, now is the time to be ruthless.   If you have a tendency to rant out loud or in your head nonstop, go ahead and put down on paper all that you're telling yourself.   Now is not the time to be 'spiritual and enlightened'; see how closely you can document the mental chatter verbatim.   Is there more? Write until you feel complete.

STEP 2: APPRECIATION

Now, write through all that you appreciate about your partner. Depending on how much appreciation practice you've had, this can be easy and enjoyable, or it can be excruciating. Many of us haven't deliberately practiced appreciation and our gratitude muscles are puny.   Don't give in to the temptation to blame your partner if you can't think of anything to appreciate.   Keep looking until you've found at least five large or small things you enjoy, admire, appreciate, respect or love about your partner. Find more if you want to! More is better.

STEP 3: WHAT DO I DESIRE?

Set the above lists aside and clear your mind. Now, write out what YOU want to experience in partnership. Don't hold yourself to the limitations you see in your current partnership (and don't assume that if you want something that your partnership can't provide then it means you're being unfaithful). Be expansive. This is about you, not them. This is your turn to get in touch with where that sparkle comes alive in you. Listen to your deepest yearnings. Resist that temptation to blame someone else for what is missing in your own life; that mental addiction siphons off the very creative energy needed to manifest your amazing reality right now. Discipline yourself to focus on what you desire and let go, at the moment, of knowing exactly how your desires will manifest. Let go of what you think you **should** want. Don't limit yourself to what you believe is available. Feel into your body, let yourself simply notice what you **do** want.

STEP 4: WHAT DO I VALUE?

Return to your writing in Step 1 where you explored all your concerns. Take your time and re-read them. They are important messages to you from your inner self. Explore what your concerns tell you about what you value.

STEP 5: SOULPATH IT

Now, do a basic SoulPath Clearing, either with your partner or by yourself and receive support in sweeping away all that keeps you from manifesting your deepest desires. You may be surprised at how readily available joy and love and profound connection are, in abundance, right now from where you stand.

Chapter 21

Continuing the love journey

I took in Nature's words about intimate partnership and they felt right, but also very alien to my programming, and it was difficult for me to retain anything we discussed longer than a day at a time. As I explored this new relationship with D__, I leaned heavily on my regular visits with Nature to help me stay centered and grounded.

Nature recommended that I spend plenty of time in meditation, opening my conscious awareness to God's presence, and I did. To my surprise and delight, every time I spent more than a few breaths in a state of blissful communion with God, I would notice D__'s etheric presence join me. It was fun, but was it OK? My childhood religious training screamed "sacrilege!"

I decided to get God's perspective on the matter.

ഗൡ

Me: *Hi God.*

God: *Hello Beloved.*

Me: *Mmmm. I could sit all day in your presence.*

God: *You do.*

Me: *Wondering why I feel such a yearning to be with D__.
Worried somehow that it's taking away from my
relationship with You.*

God: *Poppycock.*

Me: *As I wrote that I felt the twist in the field. Will you help
me untwist?*

God: *See if you can untwist yourself. I'll be right here if it
gets too gnarly.*

Me: *Soooo. My connection with D__ . . . feels like being
with you.*

God: *It's one and the same.*

Me: *OK. So. I feel vulnerable about . . . what? Scared of —*
what? I want to be with him, physically, to hold his hand,
to hug him, to touch his face. To love him. This yearning is
very big. I don't understand it.

God: *You ARE touching his face, making love with him,*
holding him. You are doing all of that through me.

Me: *Are you saying that a long distance relationship is*
enough, that we don't need to be in the same place?

God: *I'm saying that there is no such thing as distance.*

You wonder what will happen when you are in the
physical together, when difficulties arise and you tackle
them together (or don't). You wonder how you might grow
when in the same physical proximity.

You also seek relief for the places where you don't know
how to Source me in your life. Money, love, security during
the changes ahead.

Me: *This is true. Are you saying that this is an opportunity*
to learn to love purely, without entanglement or
attachment?

God: *Precisely.*

Me: *Wow.*

God: *Yes.*

None of what you call "problems" go away just by being together physically.

Me: *Ugh. I feel . . . unsure of what to do, how to proceed. I don't know how to have all that figured out, in time to have this loving intimate partnership thing before I'm old.*

God: *Try again.*

Me: *I feel worried that if I need to have all that figured out before I am physically involved with someone, I'll never manifest a physical partnership.*

God: *Oh, you don't have to have it figured out. Just understand that to whatever degree you're still projecting your needs on another, I won't be able to come through for you.*

Me: *Oooooh. Oh. . . . Oh? Wow.*

God: *Focus on being Source, instead of seeking Source. All you need comes to you. Your Beloved will move with pleasure under your hands and mouth regardless of where you are in time and space. This is what is meant by Eternal Love. It's time to stop taking this Distance thing so seriously. Break that illusion and the others are ready to tumble over too. You are Divine. So is he. The possibilities of your co-creation really are limitless, and this "time apart" gives you opportunities that will blow your mind. So, go ahead. Make love with him. Feel him make love with you. It's all in Divine order. You can bet I'll be there.*

Me: *Thank you so much. I love you!*

Over days, weeks and months, D__ and I spent hours on the phone together, exploring, sharing about what we were interested in and what we were up to, what we were cooking and what we were working on. I found that I could talk to him openly about my relationship with Nature and God. He didn't respond to me as if I was nuts but listened and seemed intrigued.

As we got to know each other more and more, there would also be equally intense and sharp triggers that would result in disconnect and upset. I think we both gave up on the connection multiple times, but once we talked it through we would paradoxically find the fires burning stronger than before. We both noticed considerable gaps in our ability to partner well, and then somehow a bridge would form across the gap that was strong enough to dance on.

Our lifestyles and the physical distance between us made visiting each other difficult. Sometimes I wanted to throw in the towel. Every time I reached that point and began to pull away, though, it was like an inner bungee cord pulled me right back. I found a peacefulness inside and decided to just enjoy our connection without trying to make something else happen. When I went there, the sweetness between us would rise to a point that made me stop short and just breathe deeply with intense pleasure.

I had never had a connection like this before.

ℬↄℭ

Me: *Good morning, Nature! Everything seems so alive and in potential.*

Nature: *It is. Everything you see is being born anew.*

Me: *Wow. Who'd a thought it would be this way. When I started out this spring it was with images of catastrophic Earth changes, and the only cataclysms have been in my*

*own life and they've been about healing and releasing my
own defensive identity.*

Nature: *Yes. And there's more. Over the next three years
you will see something remarkable happen. Everything
will be growing at warp speed. Your relationship with D__
is part of this. You two are catalysts for amazing growth
and change. You don't know the extent of it yet but it will
unfold. Just keep doing your work.*

Me: *My work. Help me remember what that is.*

Nature: *Ask, Clear, Receive.*

Me: *Anything else?*

Nature: *No. But there are infinite creative ways of doing all
three of those. That's what you are here to explore.*

Me: *Cool. Awesome.*
*. . . . I'm also feeling this immense pressure. I feel a strong
desire to be with D__ and don't know how.*

Nature: *The "how" will take care of itself. Take this
opportunity while you are new and enjoying the newness
to let the energy unpeel you even more.*

Me: *I don't know if I've ever enjoyed a new relationship as much as this one. Our connection has a quality that renews me and I feel fed.*

Nature: *It's called Resonance, and you have it within you. Don't project that he or the relationship is your only "go-to" for it.*

Me: *I'd like this to be a long-lasting, real connection where we grow together and keep finding ways to nourish the field together.*

Nature: *You do that on the fly wherever you are, with whomever is there.*

Me: *Yes. But isn't there something bigger and better that can be achieved with an ongoing partnership?*

Nature: *Certainly, but not the ones you force into position. You have to let go of grasping.*

Me: *I know. I'm working on it. Feels like slow going sometimes.*

Nature: *You're doing fine. It takes this time. These conditions are optimal for letting go of the old, letting in the good, allowing something new to emerge. You know those seeds you planted?*

Me: Yes, in the planter boxes.

Nature: They know when to sprout.

Me: (Sigh) I feel grumpy and out of control.

Nature: This is great. It's about as near to reality as you'll get. Enjoy it!

Me: I feel . . . sometimes enjoying it. Sometimes anxious. Right now, antsy. Wanting something Big to happen. Let's see: My work — Ask, Clear, Receive. Where am I in the cycle?

Nature: Receiving.

Me: Oh, hmmm. For some reason it seems like I have issues with receiving.

Nature: You do.

Me: I have lots of ways to ask, lots of ways to clear. How the heck do I Receive?

Nature: Listen closely.

Me: Mmmmm.

Nature: You do things you enjoy. You go out, spend time in the woods. You make music. Read a book. Make home. Meditate. Relax. Bathe. Yoga. Give to yourself what you like, what you want.

Me: Well. That sounds great. I can do this. Maybe I'm better at receiving than I thought.

Nature: Another thing.

Me: Yes?

Nature: Leave your phone at home. Let D__ seek you out a little more. He needs the exercise.

Me: Oooh, I feel anxious about that.

Nature: Yes you do. But you'll get over it. Make it a game to give yourself what you want from him. Love, approval, companionship, play. Transcendental experience. Art.

Me: I'll do it. Thank you!

Closer Than You Think

Nature: You're welcome. Now GO!

Chapter 22

Expanding love's context

Liz was a friend who worked near our new home and would often pop in unexpectedly when she was in the neighborhood. Playful and outrageously creative, at 10 years younger than me she sometimes seemed light years ahead of me on the path. I was always delighted to see her and we'd sit together and eat good food and share excitedly about our learning and growing edges. The fiercely brave and honest way she met life inspired me and challenged my comfort zones. I fell absolutely in love with her. The friends she shared with me began to feed my desire for soul family. We would make music together and ride new melodies and harmonies and rhythms intuitively and freely. The music opened up a new space where a lot of people could be held. This music was nothing like the music business I had left behind me. I had been hungry for this kind of community for a long time, and had forgotten how much I needed such affectionate welcome for my deepest self.

With this growing sense of community, I found it increasingly easy to meet my needs outside of my connection with D__. This was new for me. In prior relationships, I tended to isolate when I became intimately involved with a man. Now, the man I was interested in lived far away but stayed in touch so consistently that it felt almost like he was with me, and my needs for physical companionship and friendship were met in more ways than I could count. My life was so rich and full that it all felt like dessert.

It was tricky to keep all of this in perspective sometimes. I wanted to know where my relationship with D__ was going so I could make long term plans. We sporadically discussed one of us visiting the other but plans consistently fell through, and this kept me somewhat off-balance. Nature counseled me to trust and enjoy the Mystery.

∞႖

Nature: Why do you doubt me so much?

Me: I guess I'm not sure.

Nature: Look deeper. The answer will free you.

Me: hmmmm . . . I guess I've made D__ my authority, unconsciously, and he's not here so I don't know what to do.

Nature: Precisely. Why did you do that?

Me: Made him my authority? I want to be loved by someone who will partner with me deeply and beautifully. It seemed like we were going there and then something slipped. I was ready to toss myself into the fire of the unknown, go all the way to where he lives.

Nature: To escape your life here? Is that it?

Me: Something went wonky. Partly I find myself in love with my people here and in love with him there. I don't know what to do. I thought I was willing to leave all this behind, but wondering now if that is healthy.

Nature: It looked healthy for a minute.

Me: But now I feel like a mess. And in this state, I am guessing I'd better stay put. Stay with the Known.

Nature: Your Home is Everywhere. It's inside you. You'll find Home wherever you go.

Chapter 23

Into the heart of money

One awkwardness in my new relationship with D__ that I wasn't sure how to address was my insecurity about money. As a single mom with no child support income, fears about not having enough money were usually somewhere on my mind. Running in the background was an assumption that I needed to find a man who was willing to help me fund my mothering work.

This man was emphatically clear that he was not that person. He would stay connected with me while I figured things out for myself or help me think more clearly about how I could take better care of myself financially, but he was not offering to save me from my insecurity.

This felt jarring to me but it corresponded with Nature's suggestions that I use this relationship exploration as an opportunity to face the root of my fears and release unconscious attachments to being taken care of by people and things outside of myself. Even though our connection opened me more fully to my relationship with God, this man was not interchangeable with God as my Source. I had to learn another way.

ഇറ

The dream: I'm in a richly appointed cathedral, velvet cushions and elaborate mosaics and fine woodwork. I'm sitting with the Living on the right side of a center aisle and on the left are the Dead. The Living are picking and feeding off of the Dead. I look near the back of the left aisle and to my horror I see Evil itself looking right at me. It moves slowly toward me, hollow eyes fixed on me saying in a low threatening growl, "where you gonna get the money? . . . where you gonna get the money?" As it approaches and repeats its query, my mind is in a whirl, grabbing at strategies and plans in hopes of satisfying its demands and holding it off. "That person owes me," I say desperately, knowing this is insufficient for what Evil seeks. "Wait, I have a plan --" and the plan is obviously inadequate. Evil continues to move forward: "where you gonna get the money? . . . where you gonna get the money?" The moment it reaches me all of my hopes of allaying it are gone and with crystal clarity I admit to myself what I've known all along but avoided. And I speak the name of the only thing that can save me:

"God."

And with that one illuminated syllable, the whole illusion is shattered. In an instant I'm in a ruin of a dark room, one shaft of daylight filtering through the ceiling with motes of dust floating in it. And I'm completely at peace.

ഇരുന്

In my evening meditation, I was guided to visualize positive financial flow for myself and my family. Since I sometimes feel confused about the difference between greed and authentic need, I asked to be shown what a healthy visualization might look like. I was invited to just visualize lots of it.

So I did. I saw money everywhere. Spilling out of pots and pans and under the hood of my car and on the living room floor interspersed with all the Legos. Checks lovingly made out to me in gratitude for the gifts I give. I felt a big wad of it in my back pocket and opened my purse and there was more.

"How am I doing?" I asked. "Fantastic!" Nature said.

Then, I felt and 'saw' money in my hands. I noticed first a feeling of warm gratitude and appreciation, and then my feelings took a dive into something that felt painful. I started to backpedal, judging myself for not being able to hold a positive vibe consistently.

Then something inside me said, 'Stop. Listen.' And I realized that this was a part of the meditation too. It occurred to me that in addition to asking for what I wanted, I needed to also listen for what Money had to say to me. And so I listened, and this is what I heard.

Money is a manifestation of our collective Mind.

Before I send Money back out in the world, I receive it fully, allowing it to seep into the crevices of lack consciousness.   Let it rest against the experience of need.

I take it in and I listen to what it has to tell me about the Heart of the world; where we still suffer and believe we are separate and must struggle to survive.   I notice where I, too, may be grasping for something certain in this wild tumble of existence.

I ask Money, "What do YOU want?"

And I listen.

I heard that Money is weary of being used as a plaything for wicked and cruel appetites. It grieves for the pain that it has seen and been a part in. It feels a restless ache for an awakened humanity to liberate it, rejoining the fragments of the once-sacred Hoop and making it whole again.

I heard that Money yearns for a truly grateful heart to receive it, and with kindness to give it.

I heard that Money wants me to know that it is only one small part of an endless flow of abundance, which I experience as my true nature when I wake up and remember Who I am.

Yesterday afternoon, I received a check from a client in the mail, a deposit on a brand new website that I will build for her business. Since it was Saturday and banks were closed, I set it aside and went on with my day.

After my meditation, I picked the check up again. I listened. I could hear a wordless yearning that my client had for this investment to be a meaningful one, to support her own life's work to be liberated so that she could do what she came here to do in beautiful and powerful ways. I felt the vulnerability of showing up in life with a unique gift, full of hope and passion. I felt a strengthening of my resolve and commitment that this flow of abundance between us would be indeed a rich one.   And that the Sacred Hoop of giving and receiving is honored more and more deeply as a continuous flow; they are one and the same.

In gratitude.

Aho.

Chapter 24

Home again

Looking into the maw
of a great loneliness

I respond by
throwing myself into the misery
with enthusiasm.

I am not masochistic.

Something in me whispered
"You think loneliness is a sleep state
But she calls you to a greater awakening."

Closer Than You Think

And I, being a consciousness junkie, leapt in.

Here I find
the empty kiva
that echoes of lost tribes,

The abandoned stone circle
that used show us how to be
Human.

I call back through the ages.
Where have my People gone?

You and I were not made
to subsist like this
on the edges of each other's minds.

We were made to warp and weave
The aching to be One
Leading us half mad through life
Accepting myths like
"love is scarce"

when we were made to be inseparable.

I am sorry honey, but you have become a slave to the autism of
society. It is not your neurosis, but your sanity that roars
like a great beast in the night, denying you sleep, until you answer
with true connection.

I am pounding on my heart drum.
I am calling,
Calling us
Home.

ഉറ

MAY 26, 2015

I am one year into my journey.   Back in the RV for two months
now, beginning at the first of April (no fooling).

The first month and a half nearly leveled me.

Parked in my sister Tasha's driveway for the still-cold nights, feeling
untethered and ungrounded, I found myself on an inner journey
rather than an outer one.   The RV was my placental interface as I
was wrapped in a womb, re-living painfully twisted early
beginnings.   My trauma therapist sister Toni, visiting from Mexico,
brought me the gift of her skills to help release and integrate old
traumas.   One session with her reveals a childhood hurt that I had

deliberately hidden from myself, out of my inability to process or understand it at the time. A crack in a hard façade. Crazy grief and pain seeping out.

I keep breathing. I know I am in the process of going un-numb.

And this sounds dumb maybe but I didn't really know how bad it would hurt.

Toni returns to Mexico before our work is complete. I'm not sure why but it didn't occur to me to insist on staying with the process via Skype. Traveling stunned through the days, trying to function well enough to pull together enough money to pay my bills. Failing. The mortgage company calling every other day (Cindy, Linda and Donna. I know the ladies by name now), making sure I knew that they knew that I was missing my payments. And the other bills that don't have financial answers yet, but aren't making a fuss (but will).

Echoes of last year's intuitive whispered warnings about Earth changes reverberate in my inner space. I'm taking them with a grain of salt this time, but part of me would welcome such a release.

The children want to know when we're going to Six Flags. They did their part to earn their free tickets by participating in the amusement park's promotional reading program. Now it's my turn to take them there. But taking them there means money for gas, for parking, for amusement park food. I don't know the answer. I don't want to tell them I can't afford it. So I tell them I'm not sure, and be vague, as they are accustomed to me being. They are kind and patient with me. Ugh.

Evil says *"Where you gonna get the money?"* *"God's got it,"* I say.   But God's plan is inscrutable at the moment.

Mid-May, tenants finished their lease, moved out and I put the house on the market. Some dear friends came by the day after, wanting to know if I would rent the house to them.   *I don't know what I'm doing.   I don't know what I want.   Give me time to think about it.   Let's wait till Mercury is no longer Retrograde.*

I want to look deeply enough to find my core motive.   I expect to find something life-giving, something that will fuel me and give me new purpose and direction.   Instead, all I find is a longing to die.

I remember the Woman of Clay.   All she wanted to do was rest.   That is how I feel right now.

Let me go.

What about the Dream?

I don't care anymore.   Leave me alone.

Are the children old enough?

They've got a good dad.   They'll be fine without me.

For real?   Real mothers don't think those kinds of things.   Real mothers pull it together.   And I know that somehow I will do it.

But emotional honesty says I don't know what to do with this.   I feel stuck.   I don't feel suicidal, but fully capable of growing a cancer. I know deep down that I can manifest whatever I want. The problem is, all I want right now is to die.

Chapter 25

Grandmother speaks

I am dreaming, and in the dream I visit a Grandmother of our Tribe, She who holds healing and wisdom our souls need to grow. And I tell her that I need help, that I have lost my will to live and am dangling on an edge, needing to know if it is my time to let go and fall.

She swallows me up and from within her belly I travel through various states. The first thing I notice is a feeling of irritation and anger growing and roiling inside my own belly. I open to the feeling and it turns into life force and vitality surging through me. Aaaah! Yes! I recognize a feeling of clear, articulated boundaries snapping into place. This feels very life-affirming.

The next thing I notice is my son Elijah's face. It looks drawn and he's hunched over. In him I can feel extreme loneliness turning to self-hatred. I can feel that all that was missing was a mother who adored him. "But I do! I do adore him! I love him so much." And my heart aches for him, and I remember the many times when he wanted my attention and presence and I was too busy to give it. Trying to earn a living or fix the food or get the house in order. Never quite enough time. I'm despairing. Grandmother says dryly, "You think it's hard now, but it's a lot easier to let him know that you love him when you've got skin on." The scene changes and I witness Evil visiting Elijah and using his despair as a channel to attach to Elijah's self-image. Elijah starts to believe the lies, starts to believe that he is evil. It filters and leaks out to my younger sons. The ache turns to alarm and I shout "NO! You can't do that." I face off with Evil and guard my kids furiously. Evil can't pass through but I can't let down my guard, either.

"A lot harder to protect them when you're dead," Grandmother says bluntly.

I hold my vigilance until the scene changes again and I'm drifting in a relaxed state. Again I explore the edges and the depth of my longing to die, with curiosity, trying on the feeling one more time. It is still there, and deep.

"It's a dangerous game you're playing," she snaps at me. "Stop it."

I see my sons again and the fierce need to protect them, to be there for them surges up in me again. No way. No way am I leaving them now.

I'm willing to stay. No matter how frightened or alone I feel, I must stay. "Give me courage," I implore her. I expect to feel a lightening of the load and an infusion of confidence but instead she cackles with glee as she hurls more challenges at me. "It gets harder! Yes! It gets lots harder! but SHOW UP ANYWAY!"

"You're strong," I tell myself. And I find that I am. And in the dream life keeps being complicated and difficult and painful. But for some reason I'm able to find the inner resources to meet it, and curiously, I am feeling much more alive and engaged than when things were easier. I don't have wings, but my legs and feet and buttocks feel so strong and substantial, ready for what comes. Curiouser and curiouser.

Chapter 26

The real music inside me

The real music inside me
doesn't care about getting the notes right.
it isn't waiting for an audience.
the real music inside me isn't waiting to make it big.
It doesn't care what you think.
what it wants is to be played, surging through like hot molten lava
changing the shape of the universe, pouring like living waters
carving through canyons of soaring ecstasy.

It wants to move me, it wants to be me.

The real love inside me isn't waiting for a lover.
It couldn't care less whether my clothes or hair are right, whether
my belly is firm and taut, or rolls over the top of my jeans.
To the real love inside me, all of Creation is the Beloved.

The whisper and sigh of the wind passing through the trees rippling over my skin. The Earth rising up to hold my full weight against its luscious body, the taste of an apple bursting on my tongue. The beauty of sunlight playing on every delighted surface. The slow spin of the galaxies turning through time and space. The division of cells. To the real love inside me, the rhythmic pulse of life/death/life is the rhythm of lovemaking whether played out over a night or a lifetime or an aeon.

The real religion that breathes inside me isn't waiting for God's return:
Isn't waiting for Sunday
Isn't waiting for me to get it right
Or to be evolved enough
Or to clear my Karma
Or to master the law of attraction.
My real religion couldn't care less whether I am rich or poor.

it is stilling my mind
singing through my heart

It is loving,
it is singing,
it is birthing me
right now,

Right now.

ဆာ

JULY 2015

It has been a couple of months since I began to feel that I am so
done with living in an RV.   As much as I loved spending time at the
farm with Chris and Matt and their families, I am needing to put
down roots, to grow my own dream.   The problem is, I haven't
figured out where.   My long-distance love and I are still simmering
in sweetness, but even after a few visits to his home there is not a
clear pathway for us to live together. I am fine with loving him from
a distance for now because my life is so full of beautiful music and
dear friends, and because I know I am strong and can do what I
need to do. I will no longer wait: my roots are aching for the
earth.

I keep hearing the whispered warnings that say to get ready for
some big changes on Planet Earth, and by now I feel fairly matter-
of-fact about them. It's not 100% clear to me what readiness
means: what are we preparing for, exactly?   I just ask to be
guided and supported in preparing, and receive daily instructions
along with reassurance that everything is going well. None of it
makes sense to my rational mind but all of it points to loving deeply
and becoming more emotionally healthy and clear in my

relationships, and taking responsibility for my creations. Can't go wrong there.

Thanks to some amazing gifts of generosity paired with my new sense of determination and clarity about being here on Planet Earth, my relationship with money feels more stabilized. And I am ready to dig in!

And it is in this moment that I find it: on Craig's List, a solar powered home for rent on 30 acres, with a pond and workshop and pasture and forest. The landlord knows about Permaculture and is enthusiastic about supporting my ideas and helping me mature them.

There is one hitch: with a 30-minute drive to town, my concerns about isolation are up. It's possible that this distance will seem daunting to others and that I'll wilt and wither without the fun alchemy and serendipity I thrive on in an urban environment where people just happen to show up in the right place and time together. Nature reassures me, though, that I will be far from isolated, and that I'm encouraged to bust out of my fixed notions of what community should be like. So I decide. This is it! We took it.

Madre Tortuga sold within a week of posting her on FaceBook, to a marvelous man who will take her to Burning Man. Everything is clicking into place, all at once. We are in our new home, lugging new furniture and boxes and everything landing where it belongs. Before much more time passes, we will want to ground our intention for our new space!

ഇരു

Practice: Home Dedication

New beginnings and times of change are potent times to infuse matter with our intent. Our thoughts, words and emotions come together to form a matrix that influence what we experience and manifest. If we choose our thoughts and words and emotions consciously, the matrix will be supportive to our intent. If we are haphazard or fuzzy in our intent, the matrix will hold that as well. The Home Dedication is a simple but great way to help ground your intention for your life when you've moved to a new location, or when you realize that your core intentions for your lifestyle have changed and need to be refreshed. So the first step of a Home Dedication is to take the time to get clear on what your intention is for your home space, and then create a declaration that crystallizes the essence of your intention.

Here is a sample declaration for a Home Dedication I once did:

My time here is for reclaiming my inner beauty, liberating creative expression, loving the unlovable, healing, growth, transformation; manifesting money as guided; building greater resilience in my connection with mySelf, and preparing me for my next steps on the Journey Home.

Reviewing it and looking in retrospect, I am struck by how beautifully this intent manifested.   For my new home, this is my declaration:

During our time living in this place, I am choosing to heal inner imbalances and explore healthy co-creation between masculine and feminine as well as between me and Nature; to live sustainably and to move toward living regeneratively; and to thrive financially and in all other forms of abundance.

Now it's your turn. Ask yourself clarifying questions to unveil your intent for your space and write your answers down.   You may consider some of my questions below, or you may have questions of your own.   Write down your answers as clearly as you can.

What do I wish to experience in my living space?   What am I grateful for, that I wish to bring forward into the future? What am I glad to leave behind?   What would I

like my focus to be in this new space?   Where would I like
support?

Once you have reached clarity and written it down, read it out loud
to yourself or to others who are sharing your process.   You can
always change or refine it as your awareness grows, so don't get
paralyzed by perfectionism.   The main thing is to start.

After you have made your declaration and read it aloud, the next
step is to do a basic SoulPath Clearing to help you suss out and
address any areas where your intent may be blocked by
unconscious resistance.

You may keep your Home Dedication notes in a special safe place
and review them occasionally. This can help you reinforce your
intent or help you to see when your intent has shifted, so you can
recalibrate as necessary.

Chapter 27

Every available crevice

Love is carving out a place for itself in me.

Every time it comes to visit,

it seems to have grown

Its head pressed against the ceiling,

Its body filling every available crevice.

I was ready for a change anyway

so I invited Love to head the renovation team.

I should have known.

Last month it came through the place in a flood of grief

which ripped through all those walls and rafters

Closer Than You Think

sweeping away the cobwebs
and timbers
leaving a river of Living Water
running through the Living Room.

"Much better view now,"
Love said.

This month I must have seemed cold.
All of what I thought was my home
is being ravaged
with Divine Fire.

Look what you've done! I say, wringing my hands.
There is nothing left!
Yes, says Love, can we move in together now?

Warming myself by the fire
that also warms me from within
under a sky full of star friends
drinking from the rivers of tears and laughter
I realize that I, too, had felt cramped in that old cobwebby space.

I have never felt more at home.
Can I stay here always?

Closer Than You Think

Love's head is pressed against the sky
Love's body is filling every available crevice.

Epilogue

Me: *Nature.*

Nature: *Hmmm.*

Me: *Hi.*

Nature: *Hi sweetheart. I love you.*

Me: *I love you too.*
You know D__ is coming to visit.

Nature: *Yes I do. You've been waiting nearly a year for this.*

Me: *Yes. And now I feel . . . pretty good. But a little*
dissatisfied that I didn't manifest more of a cushy and

abundant welcome for him. I don't have a couch to snuggle on, like he does.

Nature: *You're comparing.*

Me: *That's right. So I am.*

Nature: *You've manifested a wonderful place to welcome him into: your own tender heart.*

Me: *I know and it is wonderful. I find it difficult to believe that I've finally connected with someone who seems to want that.*

Nature: *They all did. They just weren't as clear about it.*

Me: *Oh. I see. But to be fair neither was I.*

Nature: *Yep. He's invited you into a deeper awareness of your own heart.*

Me: *There's something a little scary too about all of this partnership stuff. I feel worried about losing grip on what I need to think about and do, to make a balanced and meaningful life for myself. Loving him, contemplating moving to where he lives, feels reckless. If the story could end just now, I wouldn't have to make any tough decisions about what I want, that could negatively affect the kids.*

I really like it here. So do the kids. I want stability for them. I often yearn for D__ in a primal, preverbal way. But I think I need to squarely seat myself before my priorities, which involve seeing to it that my kids have every advantage that I can give them. I'm just not sure what is needed since the future of the planet seems so unclear. If it is true that we're headed for infrastructure collapse, how do I begin to care for myself and the kids? How can we possibly prepare?

Nature: *The short answer is, you can't.*

Me: *And the longer answer?*

Nature: *Are you where you can focus and listen?*

Me: *The kids have been running in and out. I think we're at a pause though.*

Nature: *OK, we'll work with it.*

So, here's what you will do. Relax, don't go anywhere. Focus on what you'd like to experience, for yourself and the boys. Know that this is yours. Regardless of what seems to happen, anchor in your awareness of your desires as manifested.

Got it?

Me: *OK, let me try.*

What I'd like to experience. Is peace. Intimacy. Harmony with the Earth. An elegant way of living infused with love. Opportunities for growth, for expansion, balanced with going deeper and being close with those I love. My way of living suits me to a T. The boys, too. We're able to float down rivers, be one with the water and rocks and trees and plants and all living things.

I can't shake this feeling that what I'm describing is what happens after we die. Is this what you're showing me?

Nature: *Sort of. But you are only thinking in terms of physical death, and I am talking about death of ego. Which is what you've been working on your whole life, you know. You could easily call it ego hospice rather than SoulPath.*

Me: *Sweet. That is funny.*

Nature: *You're funny. You're the one who made me up.*

Me: *Oh that makes me crazy.*

Nature: *You're definitely crazy.*

Me: *Seriously. What are you saying?*

Nature: *I'm saying that it's time for you to stop pretending that I am some wise being outside of you.*

Me: *I feel worried about being lonely. About being unwise.*

Nature: *Let go of me.*

Me: *I . . . I'm not sure that I can.*

Nature: *You must. More awaits you. I can't protect you from life, and when you hide behind me you miss all of the fun.*

Me: *I don't know how to do this. Who will I confide in?*

Nature: *The Supreme Creator of all of Life would be fine.*

Me: *You seem more accessible.*

Nature: *Trust me. And you might try trusting D__.*

Me: *(Sigh) Does this mean no more conversations?*

Nature: *I will show up in other forms. Now GO!*

Appendix A: Gifts

In a SoulPath session, we get to see what is blocking us.   I call
these things Gifts, because each one contains keys to our
liberation.   I also notice that the person who has experienced and
overcome a trauma is a deeper, much more integrated and soulful
person than the one who has not experienced suffering, so in that
respect, a trauma is a gift that bound in painful gift wrap. SoulPath
work offers strategies to unwrap and receive the gift within.

What makes sense at an unconscious level does not have to make
sense at a conscious level.   The language of the soul is not bound
by the same logic or ethics that we call upon with our rational
minds.   If we want to bridge and access the power that drives our
lives, we have to be willing to let go of needing things to make
rational sense; we have to be willing to enter the unknown, to learn
the art of observing without adding our own twist to what we are
observing; or, to be more realistic, to notice when we're not neutral
observers.   There is so much to learn if we're willing to hone our

ability to witness the reasons why we are motivated to spin, obfuscate, dodge and distract.   Our reasons alone will tell us so much that is extremely worth knowing.

DEMANDS AND BELIEFS

Demands and limiting dogmatic beliefs are two different ways we create prisons for ourselves.   These are conscious or unconscious attempts to control the Field, which ultimately backfire and create suffering and drama. Often, the complicated and painful situations we find ourselves in have a demand or a dogmatically positioned belief at their core.   Understanding our part in the creation of these situations, paired with willingness to release our attempt to control reality, is enough to help us shift into an empowered stance and experience life more satisfyingly.

Beliefs can show up as assumptions: the basis upon which we build our reality. They can seem extremely subtle and unimportant until we get a glimpse of how they influence our perception of "the way life really is" and therefore all of our decisions. This is huge. When you find yourself saying "That's just the way ____ is", and fill the blank with whatever it is you're working on freeing up your consciousness regarding: yourself and your abilities or worthiness, women, men, life, work, relationships, reality, etc.. Take another look. Is it necessarily the universal nature of things, or is it just the way things have showed up in the past? There's no need to prove anything different; just free up your curiosity and pay attention to whether life (or anything else) is necessarily always a certain way. This simple quality of open attention is extremely powerful and liberating.

Another way to sniff out a place where you're making a demand on life is when you notice yourself using the words "should" or "must", or otherwise fighting with reality to make Life fit your idea of how it should be. Often dogmatic beliefs come in the guise of ideals that sound good, or at least very reasonable.

> *My husband should help me.*
> *Children should not hit each other.*
> *Friends should accept me the way I am.*
> *Governments should not oppress people.*
> *People should not lie.*
> *We should take care of our environment.*

No matter how right these statements sound, Should never seems to accomplish anything. Why?

These ideas render us ineffective because rather than tapping life force energy, we're fighting with it. The challenge we create for ourselves is mental rigidity and the inability to respond in ways that are actually going to make the differences we desire. Do you wish to claim your true power?

The shift is in embodying your desire.

Instead of placing responsibility on Life and other people to meet our demands, we communicate from our core.

"Husbands should help their wives" becomes *"I would like some help. Will you help me?"* It's more direct and frees up the natural urge toward willing cooperation.

"Children should treat adults with respect" becomes *"I really want respect and I'm willing to give it."* We are building social currency instead of drawing on it.

This self-responsible stance challenges our beliefs that our personal desires are unimportant (they are crucial). It can trigger feelings of vulnerability and frustration when we've experienced power imbalances, where others have demonstrated that they will ignore our preferences or use our desires against us. In these situations we may wish to choose carefully who we share our desires with, but please remember that a shift in self-talk is the most important one.

Communicating from our core in some situations may trigger grief. When *"friends should accept me the way I am"* turns into *"will you accept me as I am?"*, we may receive the acceptance we desire, or we may get to grieve the reality that acceptance isn't available from those we wanted it from.   This is not failure, though.   Sometimes grieving is the necessary step in pulling us out of paralysis. "*Governments should not oppress people*" fails to acknowledge that sometimes governments do become oppressive.   When the self-talk becomes "*I desire a government that works for the good of the people*", we then get to face our decision, or indecision, to be part of creating that reality.

The game of shifting from calcified belief systems can sometimes seem subtle or nit-picky, but it can make the difference between a parched inner desert and an inner world drenched in meaning and richness as we are drawing to us the experiences we really wish to have.   A "Should" holds us separate from such messy feelings, which can feel safe, but cuts us off from our true power to create consciously and from our deepest longings.

DECISIONS, AGREEMENTS & CONTRACTS

Decisions, agreements and contracts are three types of dynamics we set in motion, consciously or unconsciously, that continue to influence how we experience our lives long after. Even if we've forgotten making them, even if they are no longer relevant, even if they sabotage our dreams and plans, they are in effect at the unconscious level until we consciously and deliberately address them.

Following are some ways to meet the energy of a decision, agreement or life contract that can help you move in your life in a more deliberate and empowered way. Please note that I'm not saying that there's one right way to address agreements, decisions or contracts; the first thing that must be done is to listen as deeply as possible, to fully understand what we've decided or agreed to, and why. It's important to acknowledge that we did the best we could at the time we did it, and that if we have learned more and are ready to choose differently, that respect and honor is given to what happened in the past, in order to have a strong foundation to build on. Once we truly comprehend our agreements and decisions and contracts, we'll have vital information that will tell us what is necessary for our next movement. Sometimes the next steps are dramatic and bold, releasing and making new decisions, retracting our consent to agreements, and re-writing life contracts. Sometimes the next steps are much more subtle. Always, please, move forward with an acknowledgement of our part in our creation; always with a respectful and loving acknowledgement of any others who may be involved.

DECISIONS

Decisions are an expression of will. They are like agreements and contracts except that they are made at the personality, or egoic level and we are the only ones involved in their formation.

One example of a decision is this: A small boy falls down and hurts his knee and cries. An adult relative, trying to soothe him, hushes him and tells him that big boys don't cry. The boy musters all of his will to push down the confusing emotions he feels and receives approval for his efforts. He decides that he will suppress uncomfortable or scary emotions from now on.

When the boy becomes a man, he finds himself seeking intimacy but feels overwhelmed with the intensity of his partner's emotions, and frustratingly out of touch with his own feelings. If he desires to deepen into intimacy with his partner, his first task is to become intimate with himself. This requires first an awareness of the original decision to suppress certain emotions, and secondly a deliberate and clear Parts Dialogue with the little boy inside of himself.

AGREEMENTS

Agreements are like decisions in that they are expressions of will, but are made with another person or entity. Common agreements are made with our parents; with our governments; and with the religious leaders we may have grown up with. Agreements are what hold the fabric of our social order together. If we find that our social structures are dysfunctional and we wish for positive change, we must examine what agreements we've made that contribute to this dysfunction and find ways of addressing them appropriately.

An agreement might be formed like this.

A mother feels overwhelmed with the stress of caring for others. Coming home from work tired and ready for rest, she finds the house a mess after she spent time and care cleaning it up. In her frustration she may blow up at her ten-year-old daughter whose play is at the center of the disarray, telling her that she's lazy and messy. The daughter may fight back externally, but internally, unconsciously, she agrees with her mother: "Yes, I'm lazy and messy and I cause stress." From that point on, the daughter may try to be organized and in charge of her things, but find it difficult to actualize on it, because she's attempting to act in opposition to an unconscious but powerful agreement she made. Her actions will reflect her unconscious agreement, unless extreme effort is made to override it. Affirming that our parents are right is a form of unconscious loyalty, an expression of unconscious love that children make. Growing up, we may have unconsciously agreed to be the one that holds things together while our parents are irresponsible. We may have unconsciously agreed to be the one who receives abuse while our parents unload their misery and grief on us. It happens at the collective level too. Most of us in the U.S. have been taught from a young age to pledge allegiance to a flag. How many of us as small children really understood what we were pledging and why? I would assert that this is an extremely important agreement to review and decide if we still pledge our allegiance in the same way to the same entity, or if we'd make some changes.

If your unconscious agreement was with someone who has died or who you don't desire to talk with (or who refuses to talk with you) or with an abstract entity like your community or the religious structure you grew up with, this does not limit your ability to make a desired shift in your part of the relationship. In fact, I rarely would choose to discuss this process with the other parties unless I had a close relationship with them, and I believed that discussing it would enhance our connection.

The process of freeing ourselves from unhealthy agreements can initially bring up feelings of shame and inner resistance especially if we're invested in codependent patterns; we may feel a drag on our energy that says that we're responsible for the happiness of others and don't deserve to make autonomous choices.

It is true that we do have an impact on others, but this process is one that brings life and freedom, and we do not need the permission of others to make loving choices that positively affect the quality of our lives. Ultimately, making loving choices for ourselves frees life up for others to move on their most authentic path.

To address unconscious agreements, set up a Parts Dialogue journaling session[7] between yourself and the others involved in the agreement. Take your time to really understand what the original agreement was and the role that each party played. Thank them for their contribution in your life and notice what you've lost and what you've gained, as well as how you have grown or developed (or didn't) as a result of your agreement. Make the new agreement known, or simply let everyone know that the original deal is off.

LIFE CONTRACTS

Life Contracts are an expression of our soul's intent. They are the themes we desire to explore on an expanded level, which our egoic selves may be aware of, or not. They can show up as difficulties in our lives if we're moving counter to our soul's intent; when we understand and align with our intent, everything can move with much more elegance and resonance. When we choose to engage our contracts creatively, even more personal power and joy opens up.

---

[7] See Parts Dialogue section in Chapter 1.

The first life contract I became aware of in my own life dealt with the theme of conscious relationships between men and women. It began in my early life, when I witnessed struggle between my parents. The frustration of their dynamics imprinted deeply on me. I felt anger and resentment at my mom for how she sometimes spoke to my dad.   I felt confusion and bitterness toward my dad for reasons I only began to comprehend years later. The emotional split that I perceived between them might not have been as big a deal to them as it was to me; but for me, it was like there was a spotlight on it. When I was 15 I remember listening to them fight and feeling pinned, trapped in misery, so much that I developed pneumonia during an especially difficult time when my parents were considering getting a divorce.

Because of the level of intensity that I experienced, I was highly motivated to do something different in my own life.   Hence, it became the setup of the life curriculum through which I would tackle my exploration of what is going on between men and women on Planet Earth, and how our dynamics might evolve to become more mutually satisfying.   During my twenties and thirties, in spite of my best attempts, I unconsciously played out the dynamics I'd witnessed between Mom and Dad in many ways, in relationship after relationship.   In my early 40's, after the end of a difficult 11-year marriage in which I tried and failed to do better than Mom and Dad did, I found myself with more inner resources and commitment to love myself as I explored dating again. Little by little I found myself experiencing greater levels of satisfaction and higher qualities of connection with myself and my partners. The struggle that I had experienced with my former partners, all the hard work I did and all I learned through the experience, had served as the proverbial rock and hard place that I couldn't escape, which pressed me into a new shape that I couldn't have achieved by the force of will alone.

The intensity of frustration that can accompany the recurring themes of your life contracts can be great. But I wouldn't recommend jumping in to rewrite a contract until you really understand what you were intending at the soul's level. Usually, understanding what you intended is enough to make all the difference, because when your actions are aligned with a deep sense of knowing what you want beyond time and space, all kinds of grace and beauty open up for you. The contract is in your favor, not to make your life miserable but to help you understand how to tap into greater and greater levels of fulfillment, joy, love, and awakening.

For me, when I realized that I wanted to learn how to value myself in partnership and uproot internalized oppression in all its forms, I began to have a lot more fun and to attract partners who could help me see what was in my blind spot. My partnerships became my teachers.   When difficulty arises, instead of getting defensive and shutting down I can say "thank you" and look to see what gifts I am receiving to help me open my awareness of how to love more fully and consciously.   The difference is massive.

CATCH-22

The Catch-22 is a situation where an individual has two needs that seem to conflict.   A teenager's need to belong versus her need to connect authentically.   A worker's need to keep their job versus their need to blow the whistle when they witness corruption.   A mother's need to need for personal time versus her need to know that her kids are cared for, when caregiver options seem limited.

The main challenge we meet in these situations, if we choose to compromise one of the basic needs that is presenting, is that in the collision of seemingly conflicting needs, our imagination is the casualty. Our ability to respond creatively remains in that moment of impact. Often we will play one of these situations over and over in our heads, agonizing over a choice we made even when the other obvious choice could have had equally or more significant consequences. We don't fully recover our creative power until we can look at the moment with compassion, forgiving ourselves and life and the other players.

In my experience, there are a couple of ways to extract these tightly wrapped "gifts". The simplest is just to note the needs that were at play in the situation. If the situation is current and different choices can be made, it can be enlightening to look deeply at the needs, and hear them without adding evaluations or negative judgments. The old "Good vs. Evil" paradigm is of no help here, especially when we are looking at ourselves through that filter. It is really important to be willing to see the inherent innocence in our complexity, even if it takes some searching to find the good at the core of a messy tangle. If we are willing to do this and the situation is current, we can often surprise ourselves and find creative ways to meet both needs. It was never a conflict at all, it just needed some imagination. Or, we come into alignment with ourselves and make a choice that comes from our unified will, informed by a deeper understanding of our own richness and complexity. The wonderfulness of this is that when we make choices from such an integrated place, our lives that unfold from such richness are infinitely more interesting and fill our needs much better than the alternative. To me, this is the definition of self-love and builds that elusive creature, self-esteem.

If the situation is in the past and there is no way to explore a way to meet these needs, simple acknowledgement can work wonders. I notice a sigh of relief sometimes and a re-integration of sides of an inner split, when both sides can look at each other and say, "Yeah, that was a real need.   I get it.   That was hard."   I also often see indications of a difficult Soul Contract, and find it useful to note the skills, tendencies and aversions we develop as well as life choices that we make as a result of Catch-22's. It may be that these often excruciating experiences were useful to help us expand at the soul level and accomplish something that we couldn't have come close to if we were able to experience life being easy and all our needs being met gracefully.

CROSS-PURPOSES

Cross-Purposes is just like Catch-22, except the conflicting needs belong to two parties rather than one.   I would treat these situations in exactly the same way as a Catch-22.   Obviously it's nice if the other party is available to work on this with you, but you're not dependent on their participation to significantly free up your range of motion.   Marshall Rosenberg's Nonviolent Communication is an excellent skill set to develop if you want to move powerfully with either one.

THE LOGJAM

The Logjam is what happens when there are enough blocks in a particular area that we are rendered pretty much ineffective in that area. It's the place where we will give up early, drawing from multiple past experiences to confirm our perceived inability to experience anything good in this area. A logjam can take some time to clear but the rewards are substantial.

The first logjam that I personally worked through showed up when I had been single for a while and decided I was ready to start considering dating again. I made my list of what I wanted to experience, envisioned my perfect new-paradigm intimate lover relationship, and signed up for an online dating service. As soon as I started getting attention from multiple interested men, however, I froze up. I dodged communication for a couple of weeks and when I came back I apologized and told everyone I was unavailable, then took my profile off line. "Whew," I said. "That was a close shave!"

I decided I didn't really want to date anyone after all. If the Universe wanted me to be with someone, they would just drop the right person into my lap. Otherwise, I was perfectly happy being single.

When I took it into the SoulPath context, however, I was surprised to learn that my intuition was showing me otherwise. I was

introduced to the concept of a Logjam and proceeded to receive the
help I needed to work through it.   Turns out I had a mess of
dogmatically positioned beliefs about men, dating and women that
were standing in my way; beliefs about myself and my ability to
love and be loved; mistrust of sexuality and flirting,
disappointments in courtships.   I noticed an inability to stay
grounded and present with the intensity of sexual attraction in the
field.   I noticed unconscious places where I'd bought ideas that
were prevalent in my upbringing, that "men only want one thing"
and "men can't be trusted".   I also unpeeled layers of unconscious
internalized oppression of women.   Mixed messages -- don't be a
slut; if you refuse him he'll leave and it will be your fault; my body
is all wrong -- a real woman has large breasts (mine are small) and I
have hair in some "wrong" places.   I saw that historically women
had power only if their man was powerful, so a woman's ability to
catch and control a man was paramount to her success. This set up
a catch-22 where it was not emotionally safe for the man to
express vulnerability, which ruled out authentic connection from
the get-go.   I also saw how when I was growing up the man was
acknowledged as the spiritual leader of the household.   He was
the one whose prayers more effectively made it to God. In our
family, Mom was actually the one who led in this department, but
this was held with some shame, I think. Applying this model in my
adult life led to many frustrated relationships in the past where my
partner had not had the interest and passion that I do for

spirituality, so my constant attempts to get my mate on the same page while trying to defer to his "leadership" resulted in intense conflict that destroyed our connection time and time again.

The more I looked, the more I realized that my pretense of being perfectly content to stay single was fabricated to hide a mess of grief, confusion, shame and vulnerability.

Having avoided the intensity of pure raw attraction for so long meant that I needed to edge into it gently, acclimate to the energy while staying connected with myself.   I played with flirting a little, eye contact, allowing myself to feel all the edges of the way it feels to have a crush.   It's kind of like being a teenager again, but in my forties I have the edge of knowing myself and my boundaries a little more so it's fun.

I went in with the need to free up my energy around dating, and it became less about finding the Right One (or making myself or another person change) and more about enjoying myself and exploring my life with more self-love, optimism and playfulness.   Who knows if I'll find a mate that I want to share my life with.   In the meantime I am having the time of my life and making great friends.

UNSEEN ARCHETYPES

When we grow up in any given culture, there are certain stories and examples that are commonly accepted of what it means to be a woman, a man, a child; stories about what God is and what the Earth is that help give us context for our lives and a way to quickly categorize and understand ourselves and our world, so we can get on with the business of living.

The challenge that we face during times of change -- whether collectively or personally -- is that if stories don't exist that accurately explain to us what is happening inside and around us, we may try to fit ourselves into an old story of how we 'should' be and fret that we aren't doing it well enough.   But I suspect that many of us are myth-busters, story-crashers. The more I pay attention the more I think that many of us are wired to embody a way of being that doesn't necessarily have a commonly accepted or recognized story.

What often happens is that we don't step confidently or fully into who we are because we're so busy trying to do the other, previously established stories well enough.   If we are able and willing to see the new and drop the old, more of our resources will be free to explore and live this new way, to be part of creating a new template for a new earth.

It takes a lot of courage.

It's almost universal, I think, to worry that we don't quite 'fit in', and the fear of not belonging is one of the reasons why people don't move in their lives with passion and zest. The fear of not being seen, of being seen and ridiculed, or of not being accepted acts as a tyrant, even if only on the inside. Depending on how liberated we perceive a community to be, we may feel safe to explore this freely, but in some communities we sense that we must wield our pre-established role as a badge to let people know we're safe and respectable. My former husband grew up in a town where kids suspected of being gay could be harassed, bullied or even killed. Males had to adopt a tough exterior just to be safe. In some communities, our livelihood or even our very lives may depend on fitting into an accepted mold. In other communities, the familiar social structure is held together via threat of being ostracized, the imperative to be seen as cool, and other seemingly more benign but similarly effective ways to keep change to a minimum.

Schools have social categories so kids can automatically peg who they're dealing with. Jocks, Preps, Popular kids, Nerds, Goths, and so on, all offer a place to put yourself in. What if who you are doesn't neatly fit into one of these boxes? A common theme that I see with clients in sessions is that experience of having hidden out in one box or another during school, feeling like frauds and worried that they'd be found out. So many people I talk to who seemed "popular" at school are haunted by the knowledge that no one really knew them; all the seeming success was a game that blocked them from knowing themselves or connecting authentically. Interestingly, it is often the kids that didn't seem successful socially at school who were able to understand early on that fitting in isn't everything, and that you could craft a satisfying life just being yourself.

When an Unseen Archetype shows up in your session, you may wish to look and see where you're struggling to maintain a particular role that isn't quite you.   You may wish to see where your life energy is wanting to expand into a new expression.   This new expression may be just new to your circle but can be found in the wider community; i.e. if you are a woman and grew up in a culture that accepts stay-at-home moms but doesn't know what to do with a woman who wants to be a single professional; or if your culture expects women to "do something" with their college degrees but you find yourself wanting to be with your children full time, you may need to look outside your immediate context for examples of what it is like to give life and voice to your newly emergent truth.

Who really fits into the pre-established boxes that are set out for us from our childhoods? There are so many wonderful possibilities. Men who wish to make home or express their tender side.   Women who love women, men who love men, the person who is joyful and fulfilled without a partner, those who are more naturally polyamorous, the couple who actually likes each other, the thriving artist. So much pleasure and satisfaction in life is abundantly available to us when we acknowledge who we really are and set up our lives to honor the unique life within us.

Another variation of the Unseen Archetype is when it applies to something outside yourself.   When I was growing up, the conflicting demands that I fear God and trust Him left me confused and anxious. I was pretty sure I would screw things up, so I left matters of God to the experts, my parents and their friends at church.   Later on after many years of exploration and revelatory experience I still felt self-conscious, and apt to unconsciously defer to my parents as the ones who had a direct line to God.   When I first started working with story-busting in SoulPath work, one of the first Unseen Archetypes I was offered was the idea of God as Compassion.   Another was God as Source.   Which was tricky, because I unconsciously recognized God as supplying my parents, but not me, since I now saw things differently than they do.

Reality is, the world may never acknowledge the archetype we are feeling called to embody or see.   But every person who is willing to respond to their unique selves with a "yes!" even with no external recognition is rewarded with the thrill of feeling truly alive, with lives that are rich with meaning and connection.

OBJECTIFICATION

As nasty as it can feel to be objectified, it is truly a gift to be able to name it accurately when it shows up and to understand what is driving it, so you can give yourself safe distance and address root causes accurately.

Objectification is a lid we put on over a place we got hurt in an attempt to contain the pain. To address objectification, the first step is to understand what is really going on. The second step is to understand what is needed.

Objectification of women is extremely common in the culture I was raised in. I have suspected that there's a causal link between this and the fact that in our culture, we tend to discourage maintaining a consistently strong bond between mother and child. Here, it is still common for male infants to be circumcised shortly after they're born. It is also still very common for babies to have much more physical and emotional distance from their mothers than we humans evolved to need and expect. The breast offers perfect nourishment and comfort for Baby and the act of nursing can help Mama's hormones balance and keeps the new relationship sweet and low-paced as it's forming. In the absence of these benefits, both mother and child struggle, and ultimately the whole family suffers. This disruption of bonding at an early age creates a perfect storm and feeds a phenomenon of obsessive objectification of women's bodies.

What to do about it?

In the sessions I've done where this theme has shown up, the need that presented was for reconnection with the authentic feminine: with one's own mother, with one's inner woman, with what we often associate with women: softness, beauty, sensitivity, receptivity, and so on. When we claim that place inside and allow ourselves to be beautiful, to be soft, to be vulnerable and sensitive, in small or large ways; when we allow ourselves more of whatever the feminine represents to us, we are able to receive the medicine that is needed to remove our projections and regain our ability to see others clearly and with compassion as unique individuals.

If you're feeling affected by the projections of others, the steps are still the same: understand what is actually going on, and look to see what is needed.

During the last month of living in the RV, we were parked in the driveway of my house in town, getting it ready for sale. One of the neighbors registered a complaint with the city and referred to me as "trailer trash". When I learned of this I felt deeply hurt. I did a short session where I identified the source of my trigger: frozen feelings around being unwanted and not belonging, and early unresolved hurts associated with being raised poor. The actions that were recommended were to first notice how much love there was around me from family and friends (more than I had ever dreamed possible), and then to notice ways that I could take better care of myself financially. In this session that lasted less than 15 minutes, I felt a complete perspective shift: much more happiness, and the beginnings of an ability to see my neighbor with softer eyes.

PARASITISM

A Parasite describes a role within a specific kind of relationship arrangement, not an entity or organism.   Parasitism occurs when one entity takes from another without equitable exchange, to the detriment of the one being taken from.   Parasites can be microorganisms, animals, plants, people, organizations, anything.   The key with Parasitism is that there must be consent at some level for the interaction.   Granted, the consent may be unconscious; or there may be such difficulty associated with interrupting the drain that the Host may go into denial or feel unable to shake off the Parasite.

Human Parasites usually feel entitled to the Host's resources. The Host may also believe at some level that they are supposed to allow others to drain them, or they may have sufficiently low self-esteem that the sucking attention is interpreted as a compliment. Both parties believe, consciously or unconsciously, that the Parasite can't function without draining the Host, and that the Host is responsible for the survival of the Parasite (and guilty if the Parasite is suffering). With humans, a parasitic relationship is never based in truth and is never appropriate. For both parties to grow and heal, they both need to release the parasitic arrangement. The one playing the part of Parasite needs to own their strength and honor the boundaries of the other; and the one playing the part of the Host needs to own their boundaries and acknowledge the strength of the other.

If you find that you're involved in one side or another of a Parasite agreement, it may take some courage to interrupt the negative cycle. Currently many humans are awakening to an uncomfortable realization that a good percentage of our population is behaving as parasites in relation to the Earth. This is heartbreaking for those who care, and I've seen so many of our youth become jaded about humanity. I recently learned of an organization that was calling for the voluntary extinction of humanity, based on our apparent inability to behave in a functional way in balance with the rest of life. In my perspective it is dangerous to linger too long in this despairing attitude about our kind, because our power to change our relationship with the Earth is great, and it lies elsewhere.   Parasitism is closely intertwined with, and addressed in similar fashion to power imbalances, which we'll look at next.

POWER IMBALANCES

Relationships of any kind seek balance: a dynamic and constantly evolving balance between the feminine and masculine principles and their shared co-creation, whether that co-creation is a child or a conversation or a project.

This balance always asserts itself, and co-creation is always the result, whether consciously intended, or by default.   This is true whether between human beings or within an individual and also applies to natural processes.   The primary principle that applies in any relationship is that there is balance. The issue that is up when we are perceiving an imbalance is that the balance that exists contrasts with the balance we desire.   If we are feeling stuck in a situation that involves a perceived imbalance, the secret to bringing about a balance that feels more fulfilling to us is to understand how our behavior is taking up the slack and helping to hold the dynamic in place, and to learn to value and invest our energy into those forms of our own authentic power which we are not noticing.   This can be tricky, because the very nature of this issue is that some of our authentic power is in our blind spot, and often there is secondary gain associated with staying in a disempowered state. So it will require courage and honesty and willingness to look outside the box.

One example might be that those who were raised poor experience feeling powerless to make positive changes in their lives, and they may feel apathetic and discouraged in the face of injustice and oppression. The perception is that those who were raised with more financial security are better positioned to experience fulfilling and satisfying lives. This perceived imbalance can be addressed when those who were raised poor begin to value some of the benefits that can come along with their life experiences. For example, individuals who were raised with plenty of money often were taught not to do things for themselves, but to hire others to do things for them. This positions them to dominate others financially. A hidden consequence is that if the money is removed, many of these individuals feel helpless and inadequate to life's challenges, and are burdened with a sense of entitlement that keeps them from seeing and accessing the myriad blessings that are all around them. Fear of losing their assets, beliefs that they are nothing without their financial resources, beliefs that others only pretend to love them but actually really just want their money can pose serious challenges to a person's sense of inner wellbeing and tend to encourage a sense of chronic isolation.

A person who was raised without a financial buffer between themselves and life often learns practical skills and self-sufficiency and confidence.   Through the school of hard knocks they've got a doctorate in figuring out how to make life work with minimal resources.   If you are poor, there are a lot more people in the world who share your experience, and you can feel pretty sure that those who are showing up as friends and allies are not doing so because they want your money.   When those who were raised poor begin to look around them and see how many others are in the same boat and desire change, when they leverage their social power by forging bonds of loyalty with each other, when they value their "can-do" attitude and use it on behalf of each other, when they begin to value the fact that they have little to lose, their shared power can and does change the world.

I do not mean to romanticize being poor, and I'm aware that I'm oversimplifying in order to make a point. It is not pretty, it sucks and carries with it a host of other challenges which I'm not mentioning here.   I think what I'm saying is that if we want things to change, we can't depend on those who were raised with money to make the changes because in most cases, even if they somehow wake up enough to care about the imbalances, most of them have too much to lose and are terrified of facing life without having an advantage in the form of the currency much of the world recognizes and values.   Brave and smart ones understand these

challenges that pose as privilege and work to contradict their sense
of helplessness and isolation. They can learn loyalty and generosity
and practical skills, if they're alert, and with help they can overcome
their sense of isolation and disconnect from the rest of the
world.   Many others, however, don't know how to function
without a lot of money and have less motivation to make a
shift.   The ones who are experiencing the imbalance in a negative
way are the ones who are in a position to make the biggest
changes, and they won't be able do it until they see clearly where
their strongest forms of currency lie and begin to invest in these
assets. In another context, with regards to people who live under
oppressive governments, noticing where they have a choice to give
their cooperation to the system or to withhold it makes all the
difference.

I invite you to try out these principles with regards to power
imbalances in your personal life and also as they apply to racism
and gender bias and other forms of social oppression.   If you find
yourself on the privileged side of a power imbalance and you don't
want to be there, please educate yourself about the issues that the
"other side" faces, preferably beginning by seeking to learn: reading
up on the abundance of material that comes from perspectives that
are different from yours, listening more and talking less.   If you are
willing to listen first, to set aside your attachment to being seen as
good and right for a minute, if you let go of your imagined position

that you know what is going on, you have a chance of expanding your awareness of what is actually happening, and increase your chances of being actually supportive.

Appendix B: Angels

"Angels" began showing up in my work after I had done a huge number of SoulPath clearings over the course of several years, and the work had seemed to come to a standstill.   A new opening came when I asked for a breakthrough and received it in the form of Angel sessions. The information that came forward in these new sessions seemed to have a quality of luminescence and potency that was beyond my ability to accurately describe, although I have and will continue to try. Infused with a thunderous presence and carrying within them all that was needed to make a shift that had previously seemed out of reach, these sessions were simple and gentle and beyond powerful.

Now when I say "Angels" I am not necessarily thinking of beautiful bewinged humanoids dressed in white, or cherubs flitting through the clouds. What I perceive and refer to as Angels is multidimensional, radiant, living information that has consciousness and holds specific properties such as joy, wisdom, peace, light, love and so on. "God Thoughts" is one way that I think of them. "Deva", Sanskrit for "Body of Light" is another word that accurately describes what I'm talking about here.

In these sessions, certain Angels would come into focus and would often form a pattern together that I began to refer to as an Angel Grid. My understanding is that each Grid is held in place around a particular person, couple, group or situation for a pre-determined period of time, vibrating at its unique frequency and calling forward that frequency in whatever it forms around. Never forced, just gently offered as a positive option, all that is needed to take good advantage of this gift is to be open to it.

If you have developed intuitive discernment skills such as dowsing or applied kinesiology, you can use these tools to help you fine-tune your understanding of the gifts that the Angels are bringing forward in your life. If you have not developed such skills, don't worry; the help is still there for you on an "ask and receive" basis. Direct your attention within and ask that if there is Angel help available to you in a situation, and if there is, let it be known that you are ready and willing to receive it.

If you wish to take your relationship with Angels further, there are loads of resources online and in books and classes that can teach you what you need to know. Follow your feeling of 'rightness' to help you choose where to focus your study. If you find yourself zoning out or frustrated or bored, ask the angels for help, give it a rest, and know that your interest will be answered in ways that are just right for you.

Outtakes

We are separate from the earth and each other

the same way ice

is separate from the water beneath it.

We can rise above all the other water on cold days,

days that will freeze our urge to sprout and grow and thrive.

We can insist on our differences and specialness,

our hardness and ability to be on top.

But eventually the sun comes out and the earth warms,

and it all becomes one glorious, squishy mess.

Ego says this is disaster.

Love says this is spring.

ഇൽ

On the long car ride home, I hear this conversation in the back seat:

Aidan: *Elijah! I see grass as blue as the ocean!*

Elijah: *Aidan, what you see is an illusion.*

Aidan: *Elijah! I see an illusion!*

ഇൻൽ

A sudden glitch reveals to my open eyes that I'm a prisoner and a slave in a system that has me fooled into thinking I'm free.

The glimpse is there for a second and then it's gone. But I'm now aware of it. And the system knows I see, and begins to spew clouds of confusion and fear to obscure my vision.

Love stabilizes me. A Voice speaks through my heart clearly:

> *"The greatest weapon you have is your ability to love yourself and others. Love each other as you love yourself. When you do this you become unstoppable."*

The word "unstoppable" reverberates.

Distractions come up and pull me away from my awareness of this love. I keep swimming back past the flow of mind, back into the Heart.

> *"Your Beloveds give you glimpses of God's love but don't be confused when they're not acting like God. Fiercely, relentlessly love them in all of their vulnerability and foolishness and ego. Look under the pain and confusion and see their magnificence, for they are magnificent. Stand by them and do not be confused into abandoning them."*

Yes. Yes! I will stand by my Beloveds. Their hearts are held tenderly in my own.

I am responding to fear and confusion attacks with bursts of Angel thoughts. The ego mind gets complacent and distracted by shiny fascinating busy thoughts. No, my focus goes back to my heart. Now. And now. And now. And now.

And as I keep bringing my attention back, and back, and back, singing, praying without ceasing, I hear the Voice again:

> *"The greatest weapon the Enemy has*

> *Is the belief that there is an Enemy."*

Resources

Behaving as if the God in All Life Mattered by Machaelle Small Wright, Perelandra (1997)

Nonviolent Communication by Marshall Rosenberg, PuddleDancer (2003)

The Continuum Concept by Jean Liedloff, Da Capo Press (January 22, 1986)

A People's History of the United States by Howard Zinn, Harper (February 4, 2003)

The Artist's Way by Julia Cameron; Jeremy P. Tarcher/Putnam; (March 4, 2002)

The Co-Creator's Handbook by Carolyn Anderson and Katharine Roske; Global Family (2008)

Permaculture: a Designer's Manual by Bill Mollison; Tagari Publications (December 1, 1988)

The Teenage Liberation Handbook: How to quit school and get a real life and education by Grace Llewellyn; Lowry House (1991)

www.RC.org

www.Unschooling.org

About the Author

Trina Brunk is a singer/songwriter and author with a creative mission to connect with the aspects of herself that she has lost touch with and to bring them forward in multiple media to remind herself, and others who may wish to join her, that life is so much more than we perceive it to be.